NOT NAUGHTY
BUT NICE

FRONTISPIECE

INGREDIENTS

One eccentric actress with a child who can't digest
sugar or dairy products.
One artistic, inventive cook.

METHOD

Mix well and allow to simmer for 6 months.

RESULTS

This cookbook.

LIZA GODDARD & ANN BALDWIN

not NAUGHTY *but* NICE

NO SUGAR
NO DAIRY PRODUCE
COOKBOOK

WARD LOCK LIMITED · LONDON

With Thanks to:

Sophie Alice for providing the inspiration in the first place.
Dr Joseph Luder for diagnosing the problem.
Barry Burnett for allowing Liza to be out of work long enough to write
the book.
Philip for looking after Olive.
Clare for looking after the home fires.
Stephanie for typing it.
Janet and Monica for their invaluable help.
Roy and Burt and Thom and Lisa and Neal for agreeing that we're
wonderful.

First published in Great Britain in 1987
by Ward Lock Limited, 8 Clifford Street
London W1X 1RB, an Egmont Company

Photography by Andrew Hayward
Home Economist Lyn Rutherford

Cover photographs by John Paul

Text filmset in Bembo Original
by
M & R Computerised Typesetting Ltd., Grimsby

Printed and bound in Italy

British Library Cataloguing in Publication Data

Goddard, Liza
Not naughty but nice.
1. Low-fat diet—Recipes   2. Sugar-free
diet—Recipes
I. Title   II. Baldwin, Ann
641.5'638   RM237.7

ISBN 0-7063-6586-0

CONTENTS

INTRODUCTION

This book is not trying to be a way of life, you won't be promised to lose 25 lb in a week and it's not a cranky book, knit your own tofu cardigan. What we hope you'll find is a cookbook plain and simple, but, with a difference, without milk and sugar.

The idea for this book began 10 years ago, with the birth of my son. He was diagnosed as Lactose Intolerant – one of the symptoms was projectile vomiting and he could hit a moving target at 50 yards! So we discovered the milk-free diet, not as bad as you might think.

Six years later my daughter was born and, yes, you've guessed it, was also Lactose Intolerant. No problem for us! <u>BUT</u> when she was 4 years old, Sophie contracted gastro-enteritis and had it for 8 weeks. She was very ill indeed and her body wasted away. Finally we saw a paediatrician, Dr J Luder, who suggested that she had lost the enzymes that digest milk and sugar. Within days on a milk- and sugar-free diet Sophie was fine and remains so as long as she is on the diet. It was difficult at first. She lived on meat and fruit and water. Sophie is very good about it all, she likes to go into chocolate shops and sniff the chocolate.

It was while I was scouring Health Food Shops and racking my brains for interesting items for Sophie's diet that I started talking to Ann Baldwin. Ann is a friend, who is a wonderful cook; she always does the catering for any party we have, because she makes the food look beautiful as well as taste divine. Ann also brings our dogs food once a week: green tripe (ugh); they all love it, and her; and she cuts our hair – so you see she is a very talented person, and good fun too!

Ann was full of good ideas, and fired with enthusiasm for the project of making yummy dishes for a 4-year-old.

Sophie's fifth birthday party loomed so Ann and I planned a dairy- and sugar-free children's tea party, with jelly and cakes, jam tarts and of course a Birthday Cake. The tea was a great success, among the children first; and then, while the children watched the conjuror, the adults finished it all off. A great success and no-one noticed that the food was different.

We all live on this diet now (although occasionally my son Thom and I sneak off for a Toblerone, divine!). It is easier if we all eat the same things, and I am sure much healthier for us all as sugar is not good for us. It is very difficult to live without sugar as it is included in nearly all processed food! So I have read the labels very carefully. The only thing we miss with a dairy-free diet is calcium, so we take calcium supplements.

I buy dairy- (whey-) free margarine which is good to cook with as well as eat on toast or bread. There are many brands in Health Food Shops now. Trex is good in pastry too. A wonderful firm called Whole Earth make a fabulous range of sugar-free jams as well as sugar-free ketchup and sugar-free peanut butter; it all tastes better than the sugar-full brands. Thank you Whole Earth. Marmite is a thing of beauty too, we use it in gravy because gravy brownings (including the one with the famous family) all contain sugar! Luckily the public's attitude is changing and sugar-free products are creeping into supermarkets. But beware all those 'additive-free', and 'free of artificial preservatives' labels – these products nearly all contain sugar, as that is a natural preservative! So far, only Health Food Shops have the most comprehensive selections.

So here it is; our cookbook, the result of experiments, tested and approved by our very discerning children and friends.

Writing it was quite a project! I'd go for a long ride on my horse and go to Ann's for lunch, trying out more ideas for the book, and then we'd work until dark when I had to go home and get my foals in. We were ably assisted by our four dogs who lay under the table, breaking wind a lot, or out in the garden trying to eat Ann's rabbit.

The day we made the Stollen it took us the whole day and the families ate it all in 10 minutes. The families have all been very appreciative of the results of our experiments, especially Sophie.

Scottish Duck came about because we were trying to find out whether Scotch Whisky contained sugar. We got in contact with a charming Mr. Thomas from the Ardmore Distillery who assured us that there is no sugar in whisky, so we invented Scottish Duck. We then had to have a dinner party to try it out on other unsuspecting people, who raved about it.

Another exciting day was when we discovered that fructose makes good toffee and therefore spins like sugar; we cheered and danced around the kitchen.

My mother was very funny as she said to us "I never wish to have tofu or soya pass my lips". So we gave her the Bread and Butter Pudding and Rice Pudding without revealing the contents and she loved every mouthful. If you have a family who don't like the sound of anything – don't reveal the ingredients.

The biggest ingredient in writing this book has been fun. We have laughed every day, sometimes until we cried. Finishing it is very sad for us, but we hope it will be enjoyable for you.

Happy eating!

L.G.

BRAND NAMES

We have used various brand names throughout this book, as by experimentation and a surprising lack of choice in sugar- and lactose- and whey-free ingredients we came to using the same brands all the time.

There are many milk-free margarines now on the market – watch out for whey as this is milk hidden in the majority of margarines. We found that most of the whey-free ones tasted of axle grease; we haven't actually tasted axle grease but imagine it tastes like the whey-free margarines! So we discovered **Granose Green Label Margarine** which is not only tasty on bread, it also works extremely well in pastry and cakes. The other brands we tried made the pastry to build walls with. As Ann was in the middle of her brick laying course this was quite useful for her.

We have also used **Dietade Fruit Sugar,** a powdered Fructose, throughout as it is the only fructose that we tried and was most successful – see the toffee recipe for example – we are very proud of that.

When we say stock, make sure that if you don't make your own – and who does these days except Ann? – that it is sugar-free. Only a few cubes don't contain sugar – this is hidden in a lot of products as 'caramel colouring' and any word with 'ose' at the end is suspect. We finally tracked down **Waitrose own Chicken Stock Cubes** and **Knorr Stock Cubes** of any flavour as being safe, so to save hours of ingredient reading in supermarkets please use only those.

We have said **Maison l'Heraud brandy** as this is the only brandy, to our knowledge, which does not contain sugar. Other spirits such as vodka and whisky don't contain sugar anyway. Neither does vinegar, a very pleasant man at Sarsons told me so.

Whole Earth are guaranteed to contain no sugar so are useful additions for the store cupboard. So here is our quick list of useful brand name ingredients to save you hours of reading small print, while preventing a toddler from demolishing a supermarket around your ears. Oh I miss those days of a small person helping me shop.

Guaranteed Sugar Free Products
Granose *Green* Label Margarine
Dietade Fruit Sugar
Knorr Stock Cubes
Waitrose own Chicken Stock Cubes
Trex (white cooking fat)
Whole Earth Jams, Peanut Butter, Cereals and Tomato Ketchup
Maison l'Heraud brandy
Meridian Apple Juice Concentrate
Granose Soya Milk (sugar-free)
McDougals Sponge Flour
Kikkoman Soya Sauce

Liza and Ann spinning Angel Hair (page 72).

Waitrose own brand Sugar-free Baked Beans and Sugar-free Canned Fruit
Sharwoods Creamed Coconut block – best kept in the freezer
Marmite – which makes great gravy
Epicure Garlic Purée and Tomato Purée
Waitrose own Tomato Purée
Be careful with fruit juices as we found that if the label says "concentrated from more than one country", it is bad news for our barometer Sophie. So stick to *Pure* Orange Juice.
Waitrose Own Freshly Squeezed Orange Juice
Pure vanilla essence is vital as some contain caramel
Toothpaste from Health Food Shops
Waitrose Own Frozen Puff Pastry – trace sugar

There *is* sugar in:
Most sausages and sausage rolls
Most bread and bread rolls contain milk products and sugar
Meat Pies
Ready-made mustard
Worcester sauce
All gravy brownings
Most toothpaste
Pickles and chutneys
Dairy-free ice cream
Sorbet
Ready-prepared dishes such as Bar-B-Q ribs and savoury items with sauces

Products to avoid
Nearly *all* prepared foods contain sugar – when they say "free of artificial preservatives" take care; sugar is a natural preservative and therefore is added in large amounts, so too is salt.

Some names for Sugar and Milk

SUGAR	MILK
Sucrose	Whey
Saccharose	Lactose
Glucose	Anything with cheese
Lactose	
Maltose	
Caramel	
Molasses	

Be wary of Saccharin and Nutrasweet too. The only safe one, for us, is Fructose.

COOKERY NOTES

1. All teaspoons are rounded unless otherwise stated.
2. All herbs are fresh unless otherwise stated.
3. All recipes are for 4 persons.
4. All recipes use imperial measures; but if you use metric, here are the nearest workable measures.

WEIGHT

Imperial (lb oz)	Metric (g and kg)
1 oz	25g
2 oz	50g
3 oz	75g
4 oz	100 or 125g
5 oz	150g
6 oz	175g
7 oz	200g
8 oz	225g
9 oz	250g
10 oz	275g
11 oz	300g
12 oz	350g
13 oz	375g
14 oz	400g
15 oz	425g
1 lb	450g
2 lb 2 oz	1kg

LIQUIDS

Imperial (fl oz)	Metric (ml and l)
1 fl oz	25ml
2 fl oz	50ml
3 fl oz	75ml
4 fl oz	100ml
5 fl oz (¼ pint)	150ml
10 fl oz (½ pint)	275ml
15 fl oz (¾ pint)	425ml
20 fl oz (1 pint)	575ml
35 fl oz (1¾ pints)	1 litre

LENGTH

Imperial (ft and inches)	Metric (cm and m)
1 inch	2.5cm
2 inches	5cm
4 inches	10cm
8 inches	20.5cm
12 inches (1 ft)	30.5cm

From top to bottom Satay Sauce (page 20), Oyster Sauce (page 15), Pasta Sauce (page 19).

CHAPTER ONE

SAUCES

▶

WHITE SAUCE

MAKES ABOUT ½ PINT

2 oz Granose margarine
2 tablespoons plain flour
½ pint sugar-free chicken stock or use
    half stock and half soya milk

salt and pepper
1 large egg, well beaten
1 tablespoon grated onion (optional)

Melt the margarine, add the flour and stir well. Add a little of the stock and stir well.

Remove from the heat and slowly beat in half the stock.

Return to the heat, as the sauce starts to thicken add more of the stock, stirring all the time. If the sauce becomes lumpy, remove from the heat and beat well with a balloon whisk. Once all the stock is added, simmer for 2 minutes stirring all the time. Add the seasoning.

Remove the sauce from the heat and leave to cool for 10 minutes. Add the egg to the cooled sauce, beating all the time.

Return to the heat and bring to the boil, stirring. Add the grated onion if liked.

Note To make a thicker sauce, reduce the amount of liquid and cook the sauce for longer

◀

When Liza first made Hollandaise Sauce, the instruction said pour the melted butter into the blender, omitting to say 'leave the top on' – result sauce all over the kitchen, so now known as Kitchen Sauce.

BÉCHAMEL SAUCE – I

MAKES ABOUT ½ PINT

3 oz Granose margarine
2 oz each of onion, carrot and leek
½ oz celery stalk
½ pint sugar-free chicken stock or use
   half stock and half soya milk
1 blade of mace

6 peppercorns
1 mushroom, chopped (optional)
salt and pepper
1 bouquet garni
2 tablespoons plain flour

In 1 oz melted margarine, sweat the onion, carrot, leek and celery stalk for about 5 minutes.

Add the stock, mace, peppercorns, mushroom, salt, pepper and bouquet garni. Simmer for 20 minutes, then strain, reserving the stock.

Melt the remaining margarine, add the flour and stir well.

Remove from the heat and gradually beat in half the strained stock.

Return to the heat and as the sauce starts to thicken add more stock, stirring all the time. Once all the stock is added simmer for 2 minutes stirring all the time.

Note To make a thick béchamel sauce, use less liquid.

◀

BÉCHAMEL SAUCE – II

MAKES ABOUT ½ PINT

1 blade of mace
1 shallot
4 peppercorns
1 bay leaf

½ pint sugar-free chicken stock or use
   half stock and half soya milk
2 oz Granose margarine
2 tablespoons plain flour
salt and pepper

Simmer the mace, shallot, peppercorns and bay leaf in the stock for 10 minutes. Strain, reserving the stock.

Melt the margarine, add the flour and stir well.

As before, remove from the heat and gradually beat in the strained stock. Return the pan to the heat, stirring all the time. Slowly add more stock as the sauce starts to thicken, until all the stock is added. Simmer for 2 minutes, stirring. Add salt and pepper to taste.

PARSLEY SAUCE

1 quantity (½ pint) White Sauce (see page 13), or use Béchamel Sauce (see page 14)

3 tablespoons chopped fresh parsley

Make the white sauce, adding the parsley right at the end.

◄

MUSHROOM SAUCE

1 quantity (½ pint) White Sauce (see page 13), or use Béchamel Sauce (see page 14)

6 oz mushrooms, chopped and sautéed in a little Granose margarine or oil

Make the white sauce, adding the mushrooms at the end.

►

OYSTER SAUCE

12 oysters, scrubbed and debearded
¼ pint water
2 oz Granose margarine
2 tablespoons plain flour

1 sugar-free fish stock cube
a pinch of cayenne pepper
salt and pepper

Put the oysters into ¼ pint boiling water in a saucepan, cover tightly with the lid and shake well. Cook over a high heat for about 4 minutes until the oysters are open. Strain, reserving the liquid. Discard any unopened oysters. Slice the oysters and keep on one side.

Melt the margarine in a pan, add the plain flour and stir well. Remove from the heat.

Measure the oyster liquid; if you have more than ½ pint boil until it is reduced to ½ pint. Add the fish stock cube and dissolve in the liquid. Slowly beat the liquid into the flour and margarine. Once all the liquid is added simmer for 10 minutes, stirring all the time. Add the sliced oysters and a pinch of cayenne pepper. Add salt and pepper to taste.

Serve with grilled trout or grilled halibut or anything you fancy. This is a cheap sauce if you are are in Brittany or Australia!

SEAFOOD SAUCE

1 quantity (½ pint) White Sauce (see page 13), or use Béchamel Sauce (see page 14)

6 oz mixed seafood such as flaked white fish, smoked fish, prawns and mussels

Make the white sauce and add mixed seafood at the end. If you have cooked the white fish add a little left-over liquid to the sauce to flavour.

◄

HOT CURRY CREAM SAUCE

2 oz Granose margarine
1 onion, finely chopped
2 teaspoons curry powder
2 tablespoons plain flour

¼ pint sugar-free chicken stock combined with ½ pint soya milk
salt and pepper

Melt the margarine in a pan, add the onion and sauté until transparent. Add the curry powder to the hot margarine and cook for a few minutes (see **Note**). Add the flour and stir well.

Remove from the heat and slowly stir in half the combined stock and soya milk.

Return to the heat, stirring all the time. Slowly add more of the stock and soya milk as the sauce starts to thicken. Once all the liquid is added simmer for 2 minutes, stirring all the time. Add the seasoning.

This sauce is lovely over hard-boiled eggs on a bed of rice as a supper dish.

Note It is important that the curry powder is added to hot margarine to release the aromatic oils.

◄

VINAIGRETTE SAUCE

3 tablespoons olive oil
1 tablespoon lemon juice or white wine vinegar

salt and pepper
a pinch of mustard powder
½ teaspoon Dietade Fruit Sugar

Put all the ingredients into a screw-topped jar and shake vigorously.

HOLLANDAISE SAUCE

3 large egg yolks
juice of ½ small lemon

salt and pepper
6 oz Granose margarine

Put the egg yolks in a blender with the lemon juice, a pinch of salt and a shake of pepper. Blend at high speed for 30 seconds.

Over a low heat, melt the margarine in a saucepan until fairly hot but not browning at all.

With the blender on medium, pour the melted margarine on to the egg yolks in a very slow but steady trickle.

When all the margarine has been added, blend at high speed for 15 seconds. Pour into a bowl and serve immediately.

▲

MAYONNAISE

MAKES ABOUT 1 PINT

3 large egg yolks
1 scant teaspoon salt
½ teaspoon pepper
1 teaspoon mustard powder

¼ pint olive oil
½ pint sunflower oil
about 3 tablespoons white wine
    vinegar or lemon juice

Put the egg yolks, salt, pepper and mustard into a bowl and whisk at high speed until light and moussy.

Add the oil, ½ teaspoon at a time, whisking well with each addition.

Finally add the white wine vinegar. If the mayonnaise is too thick, add a little boiling water.

Variations

Orange Mayonnaise Use only 1 tablespoon vinegar and add 2 tablespoons freshly squeezed orange juice and 1 teaspoon freshly grated orange rind.

Tartare Sauce Add 5 chopped gherkins, 3 teaspoons chopped capers and 1 dessertspoon chopped onion or shallot to the basic mayonnaise.

Cocktail Sauce Add 1 crushed garlic clove and 4 tablespoons Tomato Sauce (see page 18) or use any sugar-free tomato ketchup.

Curried Mayonnaise Add 2 teaspoons curry powder.

TOFU SALAD DRESSING

4 oz tofu (bean curd)
2 tablespoons grated onion

1 teaspoon each finely chopped fresh
    parsley, sage and thyme
salt and pepper

Thoroughly mix all the ingredients together and leave in the fridge overnight.

◄

TOMATO SAUCE

1 lb 14 oz can tomatoes (see *Note*)
2 large onions, chopped
2 garlic cloves, crushed
2 teaspoons chopped fresh oregano
2 teaspoons chopped fresh basil

1–2 tablespoons white wine vinegar to
    taste
salt and pepper
1 dessertspoon Dietade Fruit Sugar
a little water
2 crushed Campden Tablets (see *Note*)

Put all the ingredients into a blender. Blend at high speed until smooth.

Pour into a pan and gently heat for 5 minutes, stirring all the time, to remove the air bubbles. Add the Campden Tablets and stir until completely dissolved.

Leave until cold and then pot in clean jars.

Note 1½ lb skinned fresh tomatoes plus ½ pint water can be used instead of the canned tomatoes.

Note Campden Tablets are available from home–brew wine making departments.

Variation

BAR-B-Q Sauce Omit the water and the Campden Tablets from the Tomato Sauce ingredients. Chop the tomatoes and put in a pan with the tomato juice and all the other ingredients except the fructose. Bring to the boil and simmer for about 30 minutes to give a good rich sauce. Add fructose to taste. This makes quite a large quantity and freezes well.

▲

"What is food to one man is bitter poison to others"
Lucretius

BREAD SAUCE

1 large onion, finely chopped
¾ pint soya milk
10 cloves

about 6 oz fresh breadcrumbs
salt and pepper

Add the onion to the milk in a pan. If you have a tea infuser, put the cloves in this and add to the milk; if not just add them. Bring to the boil and simmer for about 5 minutes. Leave to stand for at least 1 hour. Remove the cloves and add the breadcrumbs, salt and pepper. Gently reheat before serving.

▼

POLONAISE SAUCE

4 oz Granose Margarine
1 tablespoon olive oil
1 tablespoon chopped fresh parsley
2 oz fresh breadcrumbs
2 hard-boiled eggs, finely chopped

1 small garlic clove, crushed
4 tablespoons white wine
2 tablespoons Tomato Sauce (see page 18) or use any sugar-free ketchup
salt and pepper

Melt the margarine, add all the other ingredients and cook for about 5 minutes over a low heat.

◄

PASTA SAUCE

1 large onion, chopped
1 pint soya milk
6 cloves
salt and pepper
2 tablespoons fresh white
    breadcrumbs

3 mushrooms, thinly sliced
1 tomato, skinned and deseeded
3 oz peeled prawns

Put the onion into a pan and cover with the soya milk. Put the cloves into a tea infuser or a muslin bag, add to the milk and simmer for 20 minutes. Remove the cloves. Allow the onion and milk to cool, put into a blender and blend until smooth. Add the salt, breadcrumbs, pepper and mushrooms. Simmer for 5 minutes. When ready to serve, add the tomato and prawns. Serve with shell pasta or ribbon noodles.

SATAY SAUCE

1 tablespoon sunflower oil
1 onion, finely chopped
1 garlic clove, crushed
1 inch fresh ginger, peeled and
 chopped
½ teaspoon chopped fresh green chilli

5 heaped tablespoons sugar-free
 crunchy peanut butter
4 oz creamed coconut, chopped
about 6 fl oz sugar-free chicken stock
a squeeze of lemon juice

Put the oil into a saucepan and add the onion, garlic, ginger and chilli. Sauté until the onion is transparent. Add the peanut butter and stir over the heat for a few moments. Add the creamed coconut and the stock. Bring to the boil and finish with a squeeze of lemon juice.

◄

HOI SIN SAUCE – I

1 large garlic clove, crushed
½ small onion, finely chopped
4 oz miso soya purée (soya beans and
 barley paste)

1½ tablespoons McPlum Sauce (see
 page 53)
2 tablespoons sugar-free tomato purée
a pinch of chilli powder

Mix the garlic with the onion. Mix in the soya paste. Add the McPlum sauce, tomato purée and chilli powder. Mix well together.

This is delicious spread on to thin belly pork slices, left for at least 6 hours, then cooked on the barbecue or in a fairly hot oven, 200°C/400°F/Gas 6 for 30 minutes.

◄

HOI SIN SAUCE – II

1 large garlic clove, crushed
½ small onion, finely chopped
4 oz miso soya purée (soya bean paste
 with brown rice)

1½ tablespoons sugar-free jam
2 tablespoons sugar-free tomato purée
2 tablespoons vinegar
a pinch of chilli powder

Combine all the ingredients and mix well.

SPICY COCONUT CREAM SAUCE

3¼ oz creamed coconut, chopped
¼ pint hot water
juice of 1 small lemon

1 or 2 chopped fresh green chillies to
  taste
2 tablespoons chopped onion
salt and pepper

Dissolve the coconut in the water and add all the other ingredients. Serve hot with fish and vegetables.

Variations

Sweet Coconut Cream Sauce Simply melt the coconut in the water, beat briskly and add 2 drops of pure vanilla essence.

Chocolate Coconut Cream Sauce Mix 2 teaspoons unsweetened cocoa powder with ¼ pint water. Bring to the boil, add the coconut and 2 teaspoons Dietade Fruit Sugar. Beat vigorously.

◄

ORANGE AND MINT SAUCE

10 large sprigs of fresh mint
1 teaspoon Dietade Fruit Sugar
4 oz boiling water

6 oz malt vinegar
1 teaspoon grated orange rind
juice of 1 orange

Take the leaves from the sprigs of mint and put into the blender goblet. Add the fructose and and pour over the boiling water and the vinegar. Blend until the mint is chopped to please the eye. Add the orange rind and juice and put into a sauceboat to serve. This sauce can be kept in a container in the fridge for some time.

◄

*We became so involved in the writing and experimenting that
real life fled into the distance so much so that Liza missed
phone interviews with local radio stations, and the only
shopping was for recipe ingredients and dog food. Families
forlornly forgotten.*

CRANBERRY AND ORANGE SAUCE

1 large orange
8 oz fresh cranberries

Dietade Fruit Sugar to taste

Squeeze the juice from the orange and put into a saucepan. Add the cranberries, cover and heat gently until the cranberries are soft. The grated orange rind can be added for more flavour if liked. Add fructose to taste.

◀

RASPBERRY SAUCE

8 oz fresh or frozen raspberries, if using frozen save the juice when defrosting
water to cover

Dietade Fruit Sugar to taste
3 teaspoons cornflower blended in 2 tablespoons water
1 tablespoon Date Syrup (see page 23)

Put the raspberries in a pan, cover with water and simmer for 5 minutes or until quite soft. Add the date syrup and then add fructose to taste. Remove from the heat and allow to cool a little. Add the blended cornflour to the raspberry mixture and stir briskly. Return to the heat and bring just to the boil. Serve hot or cold.

Variations

Apricot Sauce Replace the raspberries with 6 oz dried apricots, soaked overnight, simmered until soft and blended at high speed. Add date syrup and fructose and continue as before.

Orange Sauce Instead of the raspberries use 2 oranges, peeled and sliced, then simmer gently for 10 minutes in ½ pint fresh orange juice. Blend at high speed and continue as in the basic recipe.

▶

"A wonderful bird is the Pelican
His bill will hold more than his bellycan.
He can take in his beak
Food enough for a week
But I'm damned if I see how the helican"
Dixon Laurier Merritt

DATE SYRUP

4 oz boxed dates, stones removed
water to cover

1 Campden Tablet, crushed (optional)

Cover the dates with water in a pan and bring to the boil, simmer until soft and leave to cool. Blend at high speed until smooth. Add the Campden Tablet, if using.

Note This will only keep if a Campden Tablet is added; keep in a cool place. Otherwise, use immediately.

▶

Local sayings (overheard, mostly in the Post Office) collected by us.

"I do like a nice glass of muesli with white meat"

"Palmerston cheese with pasta"

"I like a bar-b-q for kibbutz"

"marmalade has a twang to it"

"little old lettuce"

"never build a meal on a lake" (why you shouldn't *start with soup)*

"I buy my cheese from the delicate essence"

"You can tell a well bar-b-q'd sausage, you can snap it across your knee like a pencil"

"I always have decapitated coffee after dinner" – thought: is this cappuccino without the head?

Wood chip paper = Donkey's Breakfast.

Top left Asparagus with Hollandaise Sauce (page 32); *top right* Spinach Roulade
(page 31); *below* Avocado Seafood Crêpes (page 28).

CHAPTER TWO

STARTERS

▶

GARLIC BREAD

4 oz Granose margarine
1 garlic clove, crushed

2 teaspoons chopped parsley
½ French stick, sliced nearly through
    vertically

Mix together the margarine, garlic and parsley. Spread on the French stick with both sides spread well. Wrap in foil and bake in a moderate oven, 180°C/350°F/Gas 4, for 15 minutes.

◀

GARLIC CROÛTONS

3 thick slices of bread, crusts removed
3 tablespoons olive oil

1 tablespoon Granose margarine
1 garlic glove, crushed

Cut the bread in to small cubes. Put the oil and margarine in a frying pan. Add the garlic and heat until smoking hot. Fry the bread in batches, draining on kitchen paper.

CLARE'S PÂTÉ

1 small onion, chopped
1 garlic clove, crushed
2 oz Granose margarine plus extra to
  seal
2 green back bacon rashers, finely
  chopped

1 lb chicken livers
a good pinch of dried herbes de
  Provence
2 fl oz Maison l'Heraud brandy or
  more if needed
salt and pepper

Gently cook the onion and garlic in melted margarine until transparent. Add the bacon, chicken livers and herbs. Cook, stirring all the time until the livers are done. Add the brandy and simmer for about 10 minutes. Remove from the heat and season with salt and pepper. Allow to cool.

Put the mixture into a blender and blend until smooth, adding more brandy if too dry. Alternatively, if you like a coarser pâté, just mash the mixture with a fork.

Put the pâté in a serving dish. Melt some margarine and pour over the top to seal. Keep refrigerated.

▶

MUSHROOM SOUFFLÉ

½ quantity (¼ pint) White Sauce (see
  page 13)
6 oz mushrooms, chopped

Granose margarine
3 large eggs, separated

Sauté the mushrooms in a little margarine, then mix into the white sauce. Allow the mixture to cool and then slowly add the egg yolks. Whisk the egg whites until very stiff and fold into the mushroom mixture.

Put into a greased 2 pint soufflé dish. Bake in the centre of a fairly hot oven, 190°C/375°F/Gas 5, for 30 minutes. Serve immediately.

Variations

Seafood Soufflé Add 8 oz seafood such as prawns, scampi, mussels or cockles to the white sauce, in place of the mushrooms, and continue as above.

Spinach Soufflé Add 1 lb chopped, blanched spinach to the white sauce, in place of the mushrooms, and continue as above.

QUICHE

a little Granose margarine
4 bacon rashers, chopped
1 small onion, finely chopped
1 quantity basic Savoury Shortcrust
    Pastry (see page 82)
4 oz mushrooms, sliced

3 large eggs
2 tablespoons water
¼ pint soya milk
salt and pepper

Melt a little margarine in a pan and sauté the bacon and onion for a few moments. Line an 8 inch flan ring with the pastry. Remove the bacon and onion from the pan with a slotted spoon and put into the bottom of the flan. Arrange the mushrooms over the top.

Mix together the eggs, water and soya milk. Season with salt and pepper and gently pour into the flan.

Transfer the flan ring to a preheated baking sheet. Bake in a fairly hot oven, 200°C/400°F/Gas 6, for 25 minutes. If the egg has not totally set, turn the oven down to 180°C/350°F/Gas 4, and continue cooking the quiche until set in the middle.

▶

SCALLOPS AND MUSHROOMS IN CREAMY SAUCE

1 quantity (½ pint) fairly thick White
    Sauce (see page 13)
1 teaspoon sugar-free anchovy essence
4 scallops and their shells, cleaned and
    prepared (see **Note**)

4 large, fairly flat mushrooms, stalks
    removed
3 tablespoons dry breadcrumbs
fresh parsley to garnish

Prepare a fairly thick white sauce and add the anchovy essence.

Place a mushroom on each scallop shell, with the gills uppermost. Put the scallops on top of the mushrooms, coat with the sauce and sprinkle with breadcrumbs.

Bake in a warm oven, 160°C/325°F/Gas 3, for 25 minutes. Garnish with parsley and serve with lemon wedges.

Note Ask your fishmonger to clean and prepare the scallops.

Avocado Seafood Crêpes

2 ripe avocados
3 large eggs
¼ pint soya milk
about ½ pint water
salt and pepper
2 tablespoons chopped fresh parsley
  (see Note)

1 tablespoon chopped fresh chives
10 oz plain flour
1½ quantities (¾ pint) White Sauce
  (see page 13)
8 oz peeled prawns
2 teaspoons sugar-free anchovy
  essence

Peel and stone the avocados. Put the eggs into a blender goblet with the soya milk, water, salt and pepper, half of one of the avocados, the parsley, chives and flour. Blend at high speed, adding more water if necessary, to give a smooth pouring batter. Leave the batter to stand while you make the seafood filling.

Dice the remaining avocado and add to the white sauce with the prawns. Add the anchovy essence and stir well.

Cook the crêpes, one at a time, in a lightly greased frying pan. For each crêpe: pour batter into the pan to lightly coat the base, cook until the bottom is brown, toss and cook the other side. Fill and roll each crêpe as it is ready and place them side-by-side in an oblong ovenproof dish; use 2 tablespoons of the seafood filling for each crêpe. When all the crêpes are cooked, put in a moderate oven, 180°C/350°F/Gas 4, for 20 minutes. Serve with lemon wedges.

Note Freeze parsley in the summer to use in the winter, as dried has little flavour and negligible colour and is not worth bothering about.

◀

Avocado and Strawberry Vinaigrette

2 ripe avocados
8 large strawberries, washed and
  hulled

1 quantity Vinaigrette Sauce (see page
  16) plus extra if liked
4 king prawns to garnish (optional)

Peel, halve and stone the avocados. Put half an avocado on each of four small dinner plates. Slice each avocado half lengthwise, not completely, but leaving it joined at the pointed end; splay it out gently.

Do the same to the strawberries and arrange along-side the avocado.

Pour over the vinaigrette and serve. Garnish each avocado with a king prawn if liked.

SAVOURY PROFITEROLES

1 quantity Choux Pastry (see page 83)
4 lean green bacon rashers, derinded
3 oz mushrooms, finely chopped
a little Granose margarine

a little yeast extract or Marmite
1 quantity (½ pint) White Sauce (see
   page 13)
fresh parsley to garnish

Put the choux pastry into a large forcing bag with a large ½ inch plain nozzle. Grease a baking sheet and pipe 2 inch fingers, well spaced. Bake (see **Note**) in a very hot oven, 240°C/475°F/Gas 9, for about 10–15 minutes until the profiteroles are well risen and golden brown. Fry or grill the bacon until crisp, allow to cool and crumble with your fingers. Sauté the mushrooms in a little Granose margarine.

   Prepare the white sauce and add the bacon and mushrooms. Allow to cool slightly.

   Split each profiterole in half and fill with the warm sauce mixture.

   Spread a little yeast extract on the top of each profiterole and garnish each one with a small sprig of parsley.

Note Always preheat the oven when cooking or baking. It is vital that the oven is very hot, having reached the required temperature, before baking the choux pastry.

▲

CAVIAR MOUSSE

3 large hard-boiled eggs
½ quantity (½ pint) Mayonnaise (see
   page 17)
4 teaspoons lemon juice

1 large onion, chopped
salt and pepper
3 level teaspoons gelatine
3 oz caviar (lumpfish roe)

Put all ingredients except the gelatine and caviar into a blender and blend for 30 seconds. Sprinkle the gelatine on to 4 tablespoons cold water in a heatproof bowl. Place the bowl over a pan of simmering water until the gelatine has completely dissolved. Fold the gelatine and caviar into the blended mixture. Spoon into a mould and leave in a cool place to set. Serve cold.

▲

"This woman knows nothing" (Ann about Liza)

NOT NAUGHTY BUT NICE

DEVILLED MUSHROOMS

8 oz mushrooms, sliced
1 oz Granose margarine
5 oz tofu (bean curd)
2 tablespoons Tomato Sauce (see page 18) or use any sugar-free tomato ketchup

1 teaspoon vinegar
1 teaspoon crushed green peppercorns (see **Note**)
a pinch of grated nutmeg
salt and pepper

Sauté the mushrooms in the margarine and divide between four ramekin dishes. Mix all the other ingredients in a bowl together. Pour a little of the mixture into each ramekin, over the mushrooms. Bake in a fairly hot oven, 200°C/400°F/Gas 6, for 10 minutes. Serve with toast or French bread.

Note To crush the peppercorns, put them in a polythene bag and roll with a rolling pin.

▲

PIZZA

15 oz can tomatoes or 1 lb fresh or frozen
2 large onions, chopped
2 garlic cloves, crushed
2 teaspoons basil, fresh or frozen
1 dessertspoon white wine vinegar
salt and pepper
1 dessertspoon Dietade Fruit Sugar

⅓ quantity (1 lb) white bread dough (see page 101)
a little olive oil
4 oz mushrooms, sliced
slices of green and red pepper
3 bacon rashers, cooked until crisp and then crumbled
2 oz can anchovies
12 black olives

To make the tomato mixture, if using fresh tomatoes plunge into boiling water and remove skins by holding them on a fork. If using frozen, hold under a warm tap while frozen and the skins will fall off. Chop the tomatoes and put into a pan with the onion, garlic, basil, vinegar, salt, pepper and fructose. If the tomatoes are fresh or frozen, add ¼ pint water, if they are canned just add the juice. Cook all this over a low heat until it becomes very thick and soft.

Make the bread dough and either roll it out to a large circle or fill a pizza dish.

Brush the dough surface with olive oil and sprinkle over the mushrooms, peppers and bacon. Spread the tomato mixture over the top, make a lattice pattern with anchovy fillets and dot with olives.

Leave the pizza in a warm place for 15 minutes to rise. Bake in a hot oven, 220°C/425°F/Gas 7, for about 25 minutes.

SPINACH ROULADE

4 large eggs, separated
2 tablespoons tofu (bean curd)
1½ lb fresh spinach leaves, cooked
   and puréed

1 tablespoon fresh breadcrumbs
salt and pepper
a filling of your choice

Line a Swiss roll tin with silicone baking parchment. Mix the egg yolks, tofu, spinach, breadcrumbs, salt and pepper together. Whisk the egg whites until very stiff and fold into the mixture. Spread evenly on the paper in the tin. Cook in a moderate oven, 180°C/350°F/Gas 4, for 8 minutes.

Allow to cool in the tin for 5 minutes then turn out on to a clean tea towel. Spread the filling evenly all over. Roll up with the aid of the tea towel. Serve hot.

Roulade Fillings

Tuna Filling Flake 8 oz canned tuna and mix with 1 finely chopped raw onion.

Tomato Filling Sauté 1 large chopped onion and 1 crushed garlic clove in a little oil until transparent. Add 8 oz chopped canned tomatoes with 3 or 4 tablespoons of the tomato liquid. Add 2 tablespoons each of chopped fresh basil and oregano. Add 2 tablespoons Dietade Fruit Sugar. Simmer until the sauce is fairly thick. Add salt and pepper to taste.

Mushroom Filling Mix 1 quantity (½ pint) White Sauce (see page 13) with 4 oz chopped and sautéed mushrooms.

Smoked Fish Filling Mix 1 quantity (½ pint) White Sauce (see page 13) with 8 oz smoked flaked salmon or mackerel.

Seafood Filling Mix 1 quantity (½ pint) White sauce (see page 13) with 8 oz assorted seafood.

Chicken and Bacon Filling Mix 1 quantity (½ pint) White Sauce (see page 13) with 3 oz diced cooked chicken and 3 crisply cooked and crumbled bacon rashers.

Note All except the Tuna Filling filling are spread hot on the roulade.

◄

While glancing through Larousse for a laugh during a coffee break, we came across a recipe for Camel's Hump which said – marinate in lemon juice. How many lemons we wondered to marinate a camel's hump and in what? the bath?

ASPARAGUS WITH HOLLANDAISE SAUCE

6–10 stems asparagus per person, depending on size

1 quantity Hollandaise Sauce (see page 17)

Trim the asparagus stalks and tie in small bundles. Stand the asparagus bundles upright in an asparagus steamer or lie in a pan of salted boiling water. Cook for about 7–10 minutes. Drain and divide between individual plates. Serve the Hollandaise Sauce separately in a jug.

Note Also delightful is Orange Mayonnaise (see page 17).

▲

ASPARAGUS CROUSTADES

2 lb potatoes
salt and pepper
3 large eggs
2 oz Granose margarine
a pinch of nutmeg

8 oz fresh breadcrumbs
oil for deep frying
8 oz cooked asparagus tips
1 quantity Hollandaise Sauce (see page 17)

Cook the potatoes in salted water until soft. Drain and rub through a sieve. Add two of the eggs, the margarine, salt, pepper and nutmeg. Cover and allow to cool. Tip on to a floured surface and roll out to about 1½ inches thick. Cut it out into rounds with a plain pastry cutter 1–2 inches in diameter. Using a smaller cutter push half way into the potato mixture to make impressions for lids. Leave in the fridge for 2 hours.

Beat the remaining egg with 1 tablespoon water. Dip the potato rounds in the egg and water, then in the breadcrumbs. Deep fry in very hot oil until golden. Drain on kitchen paper.

Allow to cool and remove the lids with a pointed knife. Hollow out a little.

Fill with cooked asparagus tips and teaspoonfuls of Hollandaise Sauce, replace the lids. Serve cold.

CUCUMBER SOUP

1 unpeeled cucumber, roughly
  chopped
2 large onions, chopped
a bunch of fresh parsley

boiling sugar-free chicken stock to
  cover (see **Note**)
salt and pepper

Put the cucumber in a pan with the onions and cover with boiling stock. Bring back to the boil and then simmer for 10 minutes.

Allow to cool for about 30 minutes – 1 hour.

Put into a blender goblet, add the parsley and season. Blend at high speed until smooth. Serve hot or cold.

Note Adding boiling stock to the cucumber and onions helps retain the green colour.

▲

CREAM OF CUCUMBER AND ASPARAGUS SOUP

2 oz Granose margarine
1 whole unpeeled cucumber, diced
2 large onions, diced
1 garlic clove, crushed

6 asparagus spears – you can include
  the woody ends
sugar-free chicken stock to cover
salt and pepper

Melt the margarine in a large saucepan and sauté the cucumber, then add the onions and garlic. Add the asparagus and enough stock to cover. Season with salt and pepper to taste. Simmer for about 25 minutes or until all the vegetables are soft.

Allow the mixture to cool, put in a blender and blend at high speed until smooth.

Serve hot or iced, with Garlic Croutons (see page 25) if liked.

▼

*While Liza was experimenting with Ann's blender – comment
from Ann "Ifold (where Ann lives) twinned with Beirut".*

MUSHROOM SOUP

2 large onions, chopped
1 garlic clove, crushed
1 lb dark gilled fresh mushrooms,
  sliced
a little Granose margarine

1 bay leaf
1 tomato, skinned and chopped
sugar-free chicken stock to cover

Sauté the onions and garlic in the margarine; add the mushrooms. Add the bay leaf and tomato. Cover with stock and simmer for 25 minutes. Remove the bay leaf, allow to cool, then liquidise.

Serve hot with Garlic Croûtons (see page 25).

▲

VICHYSOISSE WITH CAVIAR

2 or 3 large leeks
2 potatoes
a little sunflower oil
1 large onion, chopped

1 celery stalk, chopped
sugar-free chicken stock to cover
salt and pepper
2 oz caviar (lumpfish roe)

Slice the leeks, discarding the green parts. Slice the potatoes.

Sauté the leeks in oil, then add the onions, celery and potatoes. Cover with stock and season to taste. Simmer for 30 minutes.

Allow to cool, then liquidise. Serve chilled, placing a teaspoon of caviar in the centre of each bowl.

▶

CARROT SOUP

2 large onions, chopped
1 lb carrots, chopped
a little garlic
a little sunflower oil

sugar-free chicken stock to cover
a pinch of nutmeg
1 teaspoon crushed green peppercorns
salt and pepper

Sauté the onions, carrots and garlic in oil in a pan. Cover with stock. Simmer for 30 minutes.

Cool and liquidise. Add nutmeg, the crushed green peppercorns and salt and pepper to taste. Immediately before serving, pour into a pan and bring just to the boil.

This soup is delicious served with hot Garlic Bread (see page 25).

FISH SOUP

about 2 lb fresh mussels, scrubbed
   clean and beards discarded
8 oz fresh white haddock
4 oz Granose margarine
3 tablespoons plain flour

salt and pepper
a pinch of cayenne pepper
8 oz prawns
1 sugar-free fish stock cube (optional)
chopped fresh parsley to garnish

Put ½ pint water into a saucepan with a tight fitting lid. Bring to boil, throw in the mussels, put on the lid and shake vigorously. Place back on the heat for 5 minutes. When the mussels are open, they are ready. Strain through a colander and save the liquid. Discard any mussels which have not opened. When the mussels are cold, remove from the shells, discarding the shells. Strain the liquid through muslin several times, to remove any grains of sand.

   Put the haddock into a saucepan and cover with some of the mussel liquid. Simmer for 1 minute, then cool. When cool, search for and discard any bones. Flake the fish into quite small pieces.

   In a separate pan, melt the margarine and stir in the flour. Slowly add the mussel liquid and the liquid from the fish, stirring continuously. Add sufficient water to make a soup-like consistency. Add salt and pepper to taste. Add all the fish. Add a fish stock cube to flavour if liked. Serve hot garnished with chopped parsley.

▶

NETTLE SOUP

6 oz young nettle leaves
2 oz dark green cabbage, shredded
2 oz celery, diced
2 onions, chopped

¾ pint sugar-free chicken stock
2 large egg yolks
salt and pepper
a pinch of nutmeg

Pour a large cup of boiling water over the nettles and cabbage. Add the other vegetables and cover with the stock. Simmer for 10 minutes.

   Cool and liquidise. Mix the egg yolks with a little of the cooled soup, then add to the rest of the soup. Add salt and pepper and nutmeg to taste. Reheat but do not boil.

   Serve hot with fresh bread or Garlic Bread (see page 25).

Variation

Spinach Soup Make as above, using 6 oz spinach leaves instead of the nettle leaves.

From top to bottom Garlic Scallops (page 41); Lisa's Mackerel Rice (page 42);
Plaice with Duxelles Stuffing (page 40).

CHAPTER THREE

FISH

FISH CAKES

1½ lb potatoes, boiled
a little Granose margarine
salt and pepper
2 large eggs
1 lb white fish, cooked and flaked

1 tablespoon chopped fresh parsley
a little plain flour
1 tablespoon water
breadcrumbs for coating
oil for deep frying

Mash the potatoes with the margarine. Add the salt and pepper, one of the eggs, the fish and parsley. Mix together well and allow to cool.

Tip the mixture on to a floured surface and roll into a long sausage shape. Cut into rounds about 1½ inches wide. Put on a tray in the freezer for 1 hour, or leave in the fridge for 2 hours.

Beat the remaining egg with the water. Dip the fish cakes in the egg and then roll in the breadcrumbs.

The fish cakes are best if you can leave them to stand in a cool place for 30 minutes, before deep frying in very hot oil until golden. Drain and serve.

▶

Alice B. Toklas' grandmother said:
"a fish having lived so long in water should never touch it
when dead"

FISH AND CHIPS

2 lb potatoes, such as Wiljar or King
    Edwards, chopped and left to stand
    in cold water
oil for deep frying
2 lb white fish fillets, skinned and
    boned

1 quantity (½ pint) Batter (see page
    43), flavoured with 1 teaspoon
    sugar-free anchovy essence

Drain the potatoes and dry them well in a clean tea towel. Heat the oil in a deep fat fryer until hot, but not smoking. Fry the potatoes until just beginning to show colour, drain and keep warm.

Make the coating batter. Pat the fish very dry with kitchen paper. Heat the oil until smoking. Dip the fish into the batter and then fry in the oil until golden. Drain and keep hot.

Reheat the oil until very hot, cook the chips again until golden. Drain and serve with the fish.

▶

STUFFED DEEP FRIED FISH

2 (1 lb) white fish fillets (see **Note**)
1 quantity (¾ pint) thickish Béchamel
    Sauce (see **Note** and page 14)
6 oz prawns
1 teaspoon sugar-free anchovy essence

salt and pepper
1 quantity (½ pint) Batter (see page
    43), or use a coating of egg and
    breadcrumbs
oil for deep frying

If the fish fillets are very thick at one end, place a piece of clingfilm on the top of each fillet and beat with a rolling pin until uniformly flat.

Make a thickish béchamel sauce and add the prawns and anchovy essence. Add salt and pepper to taste. Allow to cool for about 30 minutes.

Place one of the fish fillets on a piece of clingfilm, on a tray that can go in the freezer. Spread the prawn sauce over the fish and place the other fillet on top. Put in the freezer until fairly firm but not rock hard.

Cut the fish across in pieces about 1½ inches wide. Dip each piece in batter and deep fry in very hot oil until golden. Drain and serve.

Note For this dish, make sure that the fillets are both the same size.

Note Make the béchamel sauce slightly thicker than in the original recipe, so that it can be spread rather than poured.

HOT AVOCADO AND CRAB

2 ripe avocados
2 teaspoons lemon juice
salt and pepper
8 oz crab meat or crab sticks
6 spring onions, finely chopped
2 oz Granose margarine
¼ teaspoon curry powder

2 tablespoons plain flour
½ pint fish stock
1 tablespoon sugar-free tomato purée
3 tablespoons Mayonnaise (see page 17)
1 large egg, well beaten

Cut the avocados in half lengthways and remove the stones. Sprinkle each with lemon juice and salt and pepper. Spoon the crab meat into the avocado halves. Sprinkle the spring onions on the top of the crab meat.

To make the sauce, melt the margarine, add the curry powder and stir well. Gradually add the fish stock, stirring all the time. Bring to the boil, stirring all the time. Simmer for 2 minutes. Remove from the heat and allow to cool for 10 minutes.

Add the tomato purée, the mayonnaise and the egg. Beat the mixture vigorously with a balloon whisk and return to the heat, stirring all the time. Bring to just boiling. Leave to stand in the pan with a lid on for 20-30 minutes and, as the sauce cools, it will thicken slightly.

Pour some sauce over each avocado. Place the avocados in a baking dish and bake in a fairly hot oven, 190°C/375°F/Gas 5, for 15 minutes. Serve hot.

▼

ANN'S SMOKED MUSSEL STUFFED MUSHROOMS

8 large flat mushrooms
about 3 tablespoons oil
1 can smoked mussels
8 oz prawns

1½ quantity (¾ pint) White Sauce (see page 13)
freshly ground black pepper
3 oz smoked salmon pieces, cut into strips

Brush the white sides of the mushrooms with the oil. Place gills uppermost in an ovenproof dish. Put some smoked mussels and prawns on each mushroom.

Make the white sauce and add lots of black pepper. Put some sauce on to each mushroom. Pour 2 tablespoons water into the dish.

Bake in a fairly hot oven, 200°C/400°F/Gas 6, for 25 minutes. Decorate the top with a lattice pattern of smoked salmon strips. Serve.

HOT HADDOCK SOUFFLÉ

3 large eggs, separated
1½ quantity (¾ pint) warm Béchamel
   Sauce (see page 14)
1 lb smoked haddock cooked, boned
   and flaked

2 tablespoons chopped fresh chives
salt and pepper

Add the egg yolks to the warm béchamel sauce, then add the flaked fish, chives, salt and pepper. Finally fold in the stiffly beaten egg whites. Put the mixture into a greased ovenproof soufflé dish. Cook in a fairly hot oven, 190°C/375°F/Gas 5, for 20-25 minutes. Serve immediately with a green salad if you wish.

▶

HALIBUT AND ARTICHOKE HEARTS IN BÉCHAMEL SAUCE

4 halibut steaks
15 oz can artichoke hearts, sliced

1 quantity (½ pint) Béchamel Sauce
   (see page 14)

Place the halibut steaks in a greased baking dish. Place the artichoke hearts on top of the steaks. Carefully pour over the béchamel sauce. Cook in a warm oven, 160°C/325°F/Gas 3, for about 25 minutes.

▲

PLAICE WITH DUXELLES STUFFING

8 oz mushrooms, chopped
2 oz Granose margarine
2 teaspoons lemon juice

salt and pepper
4 plaice fillets, skin removed
4 green bacon rashers, derinded

Fry the mushrooms in the margarine, add the lemon juice, salt and pepper. Cool, then spread a little of the mushroom mixture on each plaice fillet and roll up individually. Wrap a rasher of bacon around each fillet and secure with a toothpick. Put the fish into a greased ovenproof dish and cook in a moderate oven, 180°C/350°F/Gas 4, for 15 minutes.

GARLIC SCALLOPS

4 oz Granose margarine
2 garlic cloves, crushed
1 lb scallops, cleaned and prepared,
   with 4 scallop shells reserved

4 oz fresh breadcrumbs
1 tablespoon chopped fresh parsley
salt and pepper

Melt the margarine in a pan, add the garlic, heat gently and add the scallops. Cook over a medium heat, for about 5–7 minutes, stirring and turning all the time. Remove the scallops and put into the shells. Add the breadcrumbs to the garlic margarine in the pan and fry until golden, stirring all the time. Sprinkle over the parsley and salt and pepper. Top the scallops with the breadcrumbs mixture and flash under a hot grill to toast the breadcrumbs. Serve with lemon wedges.

▲

COQUILLES SAINT JACQUES

6 oz mushrooms, chopped
1 onion, chopped
1 lb scallops, cleaned and prepared,
   with 4 shells reserved
1 tablespoon chopped fresh parsley
6 fl oz water

1 tablespoon white wine vinegar
1 teaspoon lemon juice
4 oz Granose margarine
3 tablespoons plain flour
2 large eggs, beaten
salt and pepper
4 oz fresh breadcrumbs

Put the mushrooms and onion into a pan with the scallops, parsley, water, vinegar and lemon juice. Slowly bring to the boil and simmer for only 2 minutes. Strain and put the scallop and mushroom mixture to one side.

Put the liquid into the pan and boil, uncovered, until reduced by one third. Melt 2oz of the margarine in a pan, add the flour and stir well. Remove from the heat and gradually add the reduced liquid. Return to the heat, stirring all the time. Bring to the boil and simmer for 2 minutes. Remove from the heat and allow to cool for about 10 minutes. Slowly add the eggs to the sauce, beating in well. Add the scallop and mushroom mixture, season with salt and pepper.

Put the scallop shells on to an ovenproof tray and spoon the mixture into each shell. Melt the remaining margarine in a pan, add the breadcrumbs and stir over the heat until they are golden. Sprinkle the breadcrumbs over the scallops and bake in a fairly hot oven, 190°C/375°F/Gas 5, for 15–20 minutes.

LISA'S MACKEREL RICE

1 lb basmati rice
3 teaspoons salt
2 teaspoons turmeric powder
6 cloves
1 inch cinnamon stick
1 onion, chopped
2 oz Granose margarine

4 oz mushrooms, chopped
1 courgette, thinly sliced
2 oz mange-tout
2 oz sweetcorn kernels
2 oz peas
1 smoked mackerel fillet, flaked
2 hard-boiled eggs and 2 tomatoes to garnish

Put the rice in a pan and rinse four times in hot water. Cover the rice with 4 pints cold water and the salt and turmeric. Tie the cloves and cinnamon in muslin or put in a tea infuser and add to the water. Bring to the boil and boil for a maximum of 5 minutes. Strain and discard the spices. Add half the onion to the rice, cover with a plate and leave in the fridge for at least an hour.

Melt the margarine and sauté the remaining onion and the mushrooms. Add all the other vegetables. Stir in the rice and finally the smoked mackerel. Keep turning in the pan until heated through. Tip on to a serving dish and garnish with eggs and sliced tomatoes.

▶

PRAWN AND ASPARAGUS LASAGNE

8 asparagus spears
salt and pepper
1½ quantities (¾ pint) white sauce (see page 13)
1 teaspoon sugar-free anchovy essence
1 egg, well beaten

3 tablespoons Mayonnaise (see page 17)
8 oz prawns
8 oz fresh lasagne, or use dried cooked
6 tablespoons fresh white breadcrumbs

Cook the asparagus spears in salted water until just tender. Drain and cut into 1 inch pieces, discarding only the very woody ends.

Make the white sauce, adding the anchovy essence. Allow to cool for 10 minutes, then slowly add the egg, stirring all the time. Return to the heat and bring to just boiling. Add the mayonnaise and season to taste.

Put a layer of prawns and asparagus with a little sauce, in a greased lasagne dish, then cover with layer of lasagne. Repeat the layers, finishing with a layer of sauce. Sprinkle over the breadcrumbs. Cook in a fairly hot oven 190°C/375°F/Gas 5 for 30 minutes or until the top is lightly browned.

MIXED SEAFOOD IN BATTER

Batter:
8 oz plain flour
2 heaped teaspoons baking powder
salt and pepper
water

a selection of seafood (e.g. prawns,
    mussels, any white fish cut into
    strips, squid, lobster, scampi etc.)

Mix the flour, baking powder and salt and pepper together. Add sufficient cold water to make a thick batter. Beat out any lumps. Coat seafood in dry seasoned flour (this is easily done by putting seasoned flour in a polythene bag and tossing the seafood in it). Dip each item into batter and fry in very hot oil until golden brown. Drain on kitchen paper.

Serve with lemon wedges, or even a Mayonnaise Dip (see page 117) or Tartare Sauce (see page 17).

▶

TROUT IN VINE LEAVES

4 oz celeriac, grated
1 oz chopped hazelnuts
3 teaspoons lemon juice
salt and pepper
1 garlic clove, crushed

sufficient vine leaves to wrap each
    fish, or use blanched spinach leaves
    or lettuce
4 trout gutted, cleaned and boned –
    leave the head and tail if desired
a little melted Granose margarine

Combine the celeriac, nuts, lemon juice, salt, pepper and garlic. Stuff the cavity of each fish and wrap each fish in vine leaves. Place in a greased ovenproof dish, brush with the melted margarine and cover with foil. Bake in a fairly hot oven 190°C/375°F/Gas 5 for 25 minutes.

Note We are lucky enough to live near a lovely trout farm, Silk Mill Trout Farm, and so we get really fresh salmon trout. They also have the most delicious smoked trout and one of our favorites, trout caviare – eat it with lemon juice, chopped onion and melba toast.

▲

"Oysters are more beautiful than any religion . . . There's nothing in Christianity or Buddhism that quite matches the sympathetic unselfishness of an oyster"
Saki

Scottish Duck with Wee Pancakes and McPlum Sauce (pages 52–53).

CHAPTER FOUR

MEAT
———

Most recipes for meat dishes are dairy- or sugar-free anyway. So we have tried to think of interesting and unusual recipes for you.

◄

BEEF BRAZIL

4 large onions, chopped	3 lb stewing steak, cubed
1 teaspoon chopped fresh oregano	8 fl oz dry red wine
1 teaspoon chopped fresh rosemary	8 fl oz strong made black coffee
1 garlic clove, crushed	1 teaspoon ground black pepper
oil for frying	salt

Fry the onions, herbs and garlic in the oil. Remove from the frying pan and put into a casserole dish. Fry the steak in three batches to seal, then add to the casserole. Add all the other ingredients and cook in a cool oven, 150°C/300°F/Gas 2, for 3 hours.

◄

Through the Ages
Foods said to have aphrodisiac qualities (just for interest sake to give you a laugh):

A – Z
Cabbage, Carrots, Celery, Chutney, Cod Liver Oil, Dates, Eggs, Fennel, Figs, Fish, Frogs' Legs, Garlic, Ginger, Goose, Grapes, Haricot Beans, Herbs, Honey, Lard, Lentils, Liver, Mackerel, Marjoram, Marrow, Marzipan, Milk, Mineral Water, Nutmeg, Onions, Paprika, Pepper, Pheasant, Pineapple, Pork, Potato, Radishes, Rice, Sage, Safflower Oil, Snails, Tomatoes, Tripe, Turnips, Vanilla, Yeast.

BEEF IN NO BEER

2 onions, chopped
2 garlic cloves, crushed
oil for frying
2 stalks of celery, chopped
3 carrots, chopped
4 oz mushrooms, chopped

2 lb shin of beef, cubed
sugar-free beef stock to cover
salt and pepper
½ oz fresh yeast or 2 teaspoons dried
   yeast

Sauté the onions and garlic in the oil. Add all other vegetables and sauté. Put into a casserole dish. Sauté the beef and add to the casserole. Pour over the beef stock and season with salt and pepper. Cook in a cool oven, 150°C/300°F/Gas 2, for 3 hours. Remove from the oven, crumble the yeast over the surface and stir until well dissolved.

Note This recipe uses yeast, instead of beer, to flavour.

▲

BEEF BURGERS

2 lb minced beef
1 lb minced lamb
2 onions, minced
1 teaspoon sugar-free garlic pureé

2 teaspoons chopped fresh basil
2 oz fresh breadcrumbs
3 teaspoons salt
1 teaspoon pepper

Put all the ingredients in a bowl and mix together with your hands. Tip on to a floured surface and shape into a long sausage. Cut into rounds about 1½ inches wide. Squeeze tightly with the hands to flatten into shape or use a burger mould. These freeze very well. Fry or grill for 7 minutes each side.

◄

While we were writing and experimenting, the four dogs (two of Ann's and two of Liza's) asked to go out and come in all the time barking in unison, to shouts of "shut up" in unison from us. When tasting time came, all four sat silently and expectantly side by side with gently wagging tails.

TOURNEDOS ROYSSINI

6 oz button mushrooms, sliced
oil for frying
4 fl oz dry white wine
4 fl oz sugar-free chicken stock
2 teaspoons cornflour

1 garlic clove, crushed
4 rounds French bread
4 oz Clare's Pâté (see page 26)
4 tournedos fillet steaks
15 oz can artichoke hearts, sliced

First make the sauce: fry the mushrooms in a little oil for a few moments. Add the wine and stock and simmer for 5 minutes. Mix 2 teaspoons cornflour with a little water and add to the mushrooms. Bring to the boil, stirring all the time. Add the salt and pepper. Keep hot.

Put some oil in a pan and add the garlic. When the oil is hot, fry the rounds of French bread. Spread each one with pâté and keep warm.

Fry or grill the steaks to personal preference. Place on the bread rounds. Heat the artichoke hearts in a pan, then place on top of the steaks. Put the tournedos on to a serving dish, pour a little sauce over each one and serve the remainder in a sauceboat.

◄

CARIBBEAN BEEF

1½ lb stewing steak, cubed
2 onions, chopped
8 oz sweet potatoes, chopped
6½ oz creamed coconut
½ pint boiling water
4 tomatoes

1 teaspoon salt
pepper
sugar-free stock to cover
1 firm banana
1 tablespoon chopped fresh chives

Place the steak in a casserole dish with the onions and sweet potatoes. Chop the creamed coconut, pour over the boiling water and stir until dissolved. Skin and chop three of the tomatoes and add to the casserole. Add the creamed coconut, salt and pepper. Add stock to cover and stir well. Put on a lid and cook in a moderate oven, 160°C/325°F/Gas 3, for 2½ hours. Remove the lid and slice the banana and the remaining tomato. Scatter over the casserole with the chopped chives.

GRANDMA'S CASSEROLE

1 lb stewing steak, cubed
8 oz ox kidney
oil for frying
2 large onions, chopped
sugar-free beef stock to cover
1 tablespoon red wine vinegar
salt and pepper

1½ lb potatoes, sliced
3 oz Granose margarine
1 large egg, well beaten
2 tablespoons dry breadcrumbs
tomato slices and fresh parsley to
    garnish

Remove all the fat from the stewing steak. Dice the kidney and remove the hard core. Put some oil in a pan and sauté the onions. Add the steak and kidney and sauté. Cover with the stock, vinegar, salt and pepper. Simmer over a low heat for about 1½ hours until cooked, stirring occasionally.

Cook the potatoes in salted boiling water. Drain and mash the potatoes adding salt, pepper, the margarine and the egg. Stir in well. Liberally grease an 8 inch loose bottomed cake tin and coat the sides with the breadcrumbs. Tip the potatoes into the tin and with the back of a spoon, mould to cover the inside of the tin, that is sides as well as bottom. Don't make the sides too thin as the potato should be ½ inch thick. Bake in a fairly hot oven, 190°C/375°F/Gas 5, for about 25 minutes until firm.

Remove from the oven and stand the tin on a small upturned basin. Gently remove the case from the tin by sliding the tin downwards, leaving the bottom attached to the potato shell. Carefully transfer the shell to an ovenproof serving dish.

When the meat is cooked, use a slotted spoon to spoon the meat gently into the case. Reserve the juice to serve separately. Garnish the casserole with tomato slices and parsley.

◄

TANDOORI CHICKEN

5 tablespoons tofu
3 heaped teaspoons tandoori powder

1 tablespoon oil
8 chicken drumsticks

Put the tofu, tandoori powder and oil in a blender and blend at high speed until smooth. Make small cuts in the drumsticks, place in a dish and pour over the tandoori sauce. Leave overnight in the fridge.

Remove the drumsticks from the marinade and cook on a barbeque or under the grill for about 20 minutes.

CHICKEN CASSEROLE WITH DUMPLINGS

1 chicken, cut into joints and skinned
oil for frying
2 onions, chopped
1 carrot, chopped
4 oz button mushrooms
sugar-free chicken stock to cover
salt and pepper
8 oz peas or mange-tout

DUMPLINGS:
8 oz self-raising flour
4 oz suet
2 green bacon rashers, chopped
1 tablespoon chopped fresh mixed
   herbs or parsley
salt and lots of black pepper
about 2 tablespoons water to mix

Sauté the chicken pieces in oil, then remove and put into a casserole dish (see **Note**). Sauté the onions, carrots and mushrooms; add to the casserole. Cover with stock and season with salt and pepper. Cook in a moderate oven, 180°C/350°F/Gas 4, for 1 hour.

To make the dumplings, mix all the ingredients together and bring to a soft dough with the water. With floured hands make into walnut-sized balls. Put cooked casserole on top of the cooker. Remove the chicken pieces and keep hot. Bring the casserole liquid to simmering point. Quickly cover the surface with the dumplings and peas. Put the lid on immediately and simmer for 10 minutes.

Move the dumplings to one side or serve separately on a plate. Pop the chicken pieces back in the casserole and serve. A complete meal in one pot.

Note It is best to use a casserole which is both flameproof and ovenproof for this dish, so you can use it both on the top of the cooker and in the oven.

◄

CHICKEN KIEV

4 chicken breasts
1 large garlic clove, crushed
4 oz Granose margarine
2 teaspoons chopped fresh parsley

salt and pepper
1 large egg, beaten
breadcrumbs
oil for deep frying

Place the chicken breast between pieces of clingfilm and beat until flat.

Add the garlic to the margarine, parsley, salt and pepper. Put a knob of garlic margarine on each chicken breast. Brush the edges with a little of the beaten egg, then fold and press together to seal around the edges. Dip in egg and breadcrumbs. Leave in a cool place for at least an hour; deep fry in hot oil until golden.

CHICKEN SATAY

4 chicken breasts, cubed
1 quantity Satay Sauce (see page 20)
   plus extra if preferred
MARINADE:
3 tablespoons Granose margarine
½ teaspoon coriander

½ teaspoon turmeric
¼ teaspoon cumin
½ teaspoon salt
1 tablespoon tamarind juice
1 garlic clove, crushed

First prepare the marinade: melt the margarine and add all the other marinade ingredients. Add the cubed chicken and leave for at least 3 hours.

Thread the chicken on to skewers and cook on the barbeque or under the grill for about 15 minutes, turning frequently. Serve with the satay sauce.

◀

TURKEY FILLETS IN HERBS AND BREADCRUMBS

4 boneless turkey breasts
1 large egg
2 tablespoons oil
1 teaspoon each of fresh chives,
   parsley and thyme

salt and pepper
1 garlic clove, crushed
4 oz fresh white breadcrumbs

Dry the turkey breasts on kitchen paper.

Put the egg into a blender goblet and blend at high speed for a moment. Very slowly trickle in the oil in a steady stream, blending all the time. Stop the blender and add the herbs, salt, pepper and garlic. Blend at high speed until smooth. Pour on to a plate.

Coat the turkey with the mixture and then with the breadcrumbs. Put the turkey into a greased roasting tin and roast in a fairly hot oven, 200°C/400°F/Gas 6, for 30 minutes.

◀

"Chewing the food of sweet and bitter fancy"
Shakespeare 'As You Like It'

DUCK À L'ORANGE

1 large duck
3 oranges
a little oil to sauté
1 onion
1 sprig each of sage, parsley and
   thyme plus extra parsley to garnish
1 carrot chopped

½ pint sugar-free chicken stock
2 fl oz dry red wine
salt and pepper
a little Dietade fruit sugar
a little lemon juice
cornflour to thicken

Remove the giblets from the duck and set aside. Wash out the inside of the carcass. Weigh the bird and calculate the cooking time at 25 minutes to the pound. Cut up two of the oranges into quarters and put, rind and all, inside the duck. Carefully prick the skin of the duck all over with a fork. Stand the bird on a rack over a roasting tin and roast in a fairly hot oven, 190°C/375°F/Gas 5, for the calculated cooking time.

Meanwhile sauté the giblets in a little oil and add the onion, herbs and carrot. Cover with the stock and simmer for 45 minutes. Strain and add the red wine. Use a potato peeler to remove some peel with no pith from the remaining orange; cut this into fine julienne strips and set aside. Cut the orange in half, squeeze and add the juice to the sauce.

When the duck is cooked remove it from the oven, cut into quarters and keep warm.

Take the orange quarters from inside the duck and squeeze the juice into the sauce. Tip off the excess fat from the roasting tin, strain the cooking juices and add to the sauce. Add salt and pepper, fructose and lemon juice to taste. Mix some cornflour with a little water and add to the sauce to thicken to personal preference.

Scatter the peel strips over the duck and garnish with a little fresh parsley. Serve the sauce separately in a sauceboat.

◀

We were given a brace of pheasants and hung them up in the utility room. Unfortunately the weather turned warm, we forgot the said birds and a few days later noticed little white wriggly things on the washing machine! Maggots! So the pheasants went in the bin!

SCOTTISH DUCK WITH WEE PANCAKES AND McPLUM SAUCE

(BEST WISHES WITH THANKS TO MR. THOMAS)

SCOTTISH DUCK

1 large duck
1 lemon
1 pint water
3 tablespoons Date Syrup (see page 23)

2 tablespoons Dietade Fruit Sugar
3 tablespoons malt whisky
3 tablespoons sugar-free soy sauce

Rinse the duck and dry completely with kitchen paper. Place the duck on a rack over a roasting tin and make the sauce. Slice the lemon into very thin slices. Combine all the other ingredients in a pan, add the lemon slices and bring to the boil. Simmer for 20 minutes over a low heat. Whilst still hot, ladle the sauce over the duck. Turn the duck to ladle all sides, making sure that the bird is covered in the sauce.

Reserving the sauce, lift the duck from the rack and hang up in a cool well ventilated place to dry. A good tip is to hang it up in a clean pillow case which is tied tightly at the top, and place a drip tray underneath. In very warm weather tie a large bunch of mint to the top to keep away any flies. Hang at least for 24 hours, or dry the duck with a hairdryer to speed up the process.

When the skin is dry, put the duck back on the rack over the roasting tin. Carefully ladle some of the reserved sauce inside the duck. Ladle some sauce over the outside of the duck and put the remaining sauce into the tin under the duck. Roast in a very hot oven, 240°C/475°F/Gas 8, for 15 minutes. Baste with the sauce, turn the heat down to 180°C/ 350°F/Gas 4, and cook for about 1½ hours.

Remove the duck from the oven and allow to sit for at least 10 minutes before you carve. Take all the skin off first and arrange on a serving dish, then carve all the meat.

Serve with Wee Pancakes, McPlum sauce and thin strips of raw leek.

▲

"For us the winds do blow
The earth resteth heaven moveth fountains flow;
Nothing we see but means our good,
As our delight as our treasure;
The whole is either our cupboard of food
Or Cabinet of pleasure"
George Herbert

WEE PANCAKES
MAKES ABOUT 24 PANCAKES

10 oz plain flour
a pinch of salt

8–9 fl oz very hot water plus extra if needed
2 tablespoons sunflower oil

Put the flour and salt into a bowl and mix at low speed, slowly adding the hot water until it comes together. You may need more water. Mix for about 5 minutes until completely smooth. Cover with a damp cloth and leave to rest for 30 minutes.

Mix again for 2 minutes, then turn on to a floured surface. Roll into a long sausage and cut off an even number of walnut-sized pieces. Roll into balls. Paint the top of one ball with sunflower oil, put a second ball on top and roll out on a floured surface until fairly thin to give an upper and a lower pancake of 5–6 inches diameter with a seam in the middle. Repeat with all the balls.

Put each double pancake into a dry frying pan and cook over a low heat for about 1 minute until cooked on the bottom, but not browned, then flip it over and cook the other side. Carefully find the seam and pull the pancakes apart. Stack them in a pile until needed. These freeze very well.

McPLUM SAUCE

1 lb fresh or frozen plums, stoned
1 garlic clove, crushed
1 onion
4 oz dried and stoned dates
2 teaspoons salt

1 teaspoon ground ginger
3 tablespoons Date Syrup (see page 23)
½ pint malt vinegar
Dietade Fruit Sugar to taste

Put all the ingredients except the fructose in a pan, bring to the boil and simmer until soft and squashy. Cool, then taste and add fructose if necessary. Put into a blender and blend until smooth. Serve cold.

THE FINALE

Prepare some thin strips of raw leek, by cutting some leeks into 2 inch pieces and then slitting lengthways with a sharp knife. Each person serves themselves by spreading each pancake with a little sauce, some thinly sliced leek and pieces of Scottish duck. Roll up and enjoy. Best eaten with the fingers.

PHEASANT IN MILK

6 cloves
2 large onions cut in half
2 pheasants, cut in half lengthways
1 carrot, chopped
2 bay leaves
a sprig of thyme
4 sage leaves

a sprig of marjoram
1 sugar-free chicken stock cube,
    dissolved in a little boiling water
1 pint soya milk or ½ pint soya milk
    mixed with ½ pint water
salt and pepper

Stick the cloves into the onion halves and put the onions in the bottom of a casserole dish. Place the pheasant halves on top of the onions. Scatter the carrot and herbs around. Add the stock to the soya milk and pour over the casserole. Season with salt and pepper. Cover with the lid. Cook in a warm oven, 160°C/325°F/Gas 3, for about 2 hours or until the meat is tender. An old pheasant may need 4 hours cooking time.

▶

ST. CLEMENT'S LAMB

1 leg of lamb
2 garlic cloves, cut into slivers
the juice of 2 oranges and 1 lemon
½ pint dry red wine

1 tablespoon Dietade Fruit Sugar plus
    extra to taste
salt and pepper
a little cornflour to thicken

Weigh the lamb and calculate the cooking time at 25 minutes to the pound. Push a sharp knife into the lamb and push a sliver of garlic into the cut, continuing until all the garlic is used up. Mix the orange and lemon juice with the red wine and fructose. Stir well until the fructose is dissolved. Find a close-fitting clean polythene bag, put the lamb, broad end down, in the bag and stand it in a basin. Pour the marinade into the bag and seal the top with a tie. Leave overnight.

The following day remove the lamb from the bag and reserve the marinade. Stand the lamb on a rack over a roasting tin. Roast in a fairly hot oven, 200°C/400°F/Gas 6, for the calculated cooking time.

When the lamb is cooked, remove from the tin, place on a serving dish and keep hot. Add the residue of the marinade to the juices in the roasting tin, put over a low heat and stir in all the sediment from the bottom of the tin. Strain the juices into a pan, add salt and pepper to taste and thicken the sauce to personal preference with a little cornflour mixed with a little water. More fructose can be added if a sweeter sauce is desired. Serve the meat and sauce separately.

LAMB WITH SHREWSBURY SAUCE

1 shoulder of lamb
6 sprigs of rosemary
salt and pepper
Sauce:
1 carrot, chopped
1 onion, chopped
2 sticks of celery, chopped
1 oz green bacon, chopped

oil to sauté
1 pint sugar-free lamb stock
2 fl oz dry red wine
1 dessertspoon sugar-free tomato
   purée
½ teaspoon chopped fresh rosemary
2 oz Granose margarine
2 tablespoons plain flour

Weigh the lamb and calculate the cooking time at 35 minutes to the pound. Stick the sprigs of rosemary into the lamb and sprinkle the outside with salt and pepper. Roast in a fairly hot oven 190°C/375°F/ Gas 5, for the calculated cooking time.

To make the sauce, sauté the carrot, onion, celery and bacon in oil. Add the stock and red wine and simmer until reduced by half. Allow to cool, then blend at high speed. Add the tomato purée, chopped rosemary, salt and pepper.

Melt the margarine, add the flour and stir well. Gradually add the stock, stirring all the time. Bring to the boil, stirring all the time, then simmer for 2 minutes. Serve the sauce with the lamb.

◀

THOM'S LAMB WITH ORANGE AND MINT SAUCE

1 rack of lamb
2 dessertspoons mustard powder
a little vinegar and water
2 teaspoons black peppercorns,
   crushed

4 teaspoons chopped fresh sage
1 teaspoon chopped fresh rosemary
4 tablespoons breadcrumbs
1 quantity Orange and Mint Sauce
   (see page 21) plus extra if preferred

Weigh the lamb and calculate the cooking time at 25 minutes to the pound plus 25 minutes.

Mix the mustard with vinegar and water and spread all over the lamb. Mix the peppercorns and herbs together with the breadcrumbs. Roll the meat in the breadcrumb mixture, patting it well in to coat.

Bake in a fairly hot oven, 190°C/375°F/Gas 5, for the calculated cooking time, basting occasionally with the cooking juices. Serve with orange and mint sauce.

LAMB KORMA

10 oz tofu, blended until smooth
½ teaspoon turmeric
2 onions, chopped
2 large garlic cloves, chopped
2 inches fresh root ginger, peeled and chopped
2 lb boned leg of lamb or lamb fillets, cubed
4 tablespoons Granose margarine

a squirt of lemon juice
½ teaspoon chilli powder
2 teaspoons mild curry powder
1 teaspoon salt
4 tablespoons boiling water
3 oz creamed coconut, chopped
1 sugar-free chicken stock cube
2 oz ground almonds

Mix 3 tablespoons of the blended tofu and the turmeric with half the onion, garlic and ginger. Put the lamb into a bowl and pour over the tofu mixture. Stir well and leave to stand for 1 hour.

Melt the margarine in a large pan and fry the remaining onion, ginger and garlic until golden brown. Remove the fried onion mixture from the fat with a slotted spoon and reserve. Add the meat to the pan and fry until nearly brown. Add a squirt of lemon juice to the remaining (unspiced) tofu and add to the meat. Add the chilli powder, curry powder and salt. Return the fried onion mixture to the pan. Reduce the heat to very low and add a few tablespoons of water if the mixture is very dry. Cook for 40 minutes, stirring occasionally.

Pour 4 tablespoons boiling water on to the creamed coconut and stock cube and stir until dissolved. Add to the pan with the ground almonds. If the mixture is too dry, add a little more water. Cook for 15 minutes, stirring occasionally. Serve at once.

Variations

Chicken Korma Use chicken breasts instead of the lamb and cook for about 40 minutes.

Turkey Korma Turkey breasts are another excellent subsitute. Cook for about 40 minutes.

◀

We actually heard of a woman who washes her bay leaves after putting them in a casserole and uses them again and again. We think that this takes economy too far.

GINGER AND LEMON LAMB CHOPS

½ pint olive oil
grated rind of 1 lemon
4 tablespoons lemon juice
1 tablespoon Dietade Fruit Sugar
1 tablespoon Date Syrup (see page 23)

1 teaspoon grated fresh root ginger
1 teaspoon ginger powder
salt and pepper
1 garlic clove, crushed
4 butterfly lamb chops

Mix the oil, lemon rind and juice, fructose, date syrup, ginger, seasoning and garlic. Pour this marinade over the chops and leave for 2 to 3 hours, turning the chops frequently.

Put the chops plus marinade into a roasting tin and cook in a fairly hot oven, 190°C/375°F/Gas 5 for about 25 minutes.

◀

CREAMY PORK WITH GREEN PEPPERCORNS

5 oz tofu
1 tablespoon chopped fresh chives
2 teaspoons green peppercorns
1½ lb lean pork, cubed
oil for frying
2 large onions, chopped
2 garlic cloves, crushed

6 oz mushrooms, sliced
2 green peppers deseeded and chopped
sugar-free chicken stock to cover
salt and pepper
a pinch of dried herbes de Provence
a little cornflour to thicken

Tip the tofu into a basin and beat well until smooth. Add the chives and peppercorns and leave to infuse overnight if possible.

Prepare the pork, removing all the fat. Heat the oil, fry the onions and garlic until transparent. Remove with a slotted spoon and put into a casserole dish. Fry the pork in batches, remove with a slotted spoon and put into the casserole. Lastly fry the mushrooms and green peppers; add to the casserole. Add stock to cover and season with salt, pepper and herbs. Cook with lid on in a moderate oven, 180°C/350°F/Gas 4, for 1 hour.

Remove from the oven and thicken with a little cornflour mixed in a little water. Swirl the tofu mixture on to the top of the casserole and serve at once.

Neal's Pork with Stuffed Apples

1 leg of pork
a few juniper berries, crushed
2 oranges

4 oz dried sage and onion stuffing,
  premixed
4 large cooking apples such as
  Bramley's, cored but not peeled

Weigh the pork and calculate the cooking time at 25 minutes to the pound. Score the rind and make sure that it is absolutely dry. Rub the cut rind with the crushed juniper berries and a little grated orange rind. Leave to stand for 3 to 4 hours. Set the pork on a rack over a roasting dish and roast in a hot oven for the calculated cooking time.

Meanwhile prepare the apples, which you can cook in the roasting dish around the pork for the last 45 minutes of the pork cooking time. Peel one of the oranges and put the segments in a basin with the premixed stuffing; mix well. Fill the centre of each apple with the orange stuffing. Run a knife horizontally round each apple. Stand the apples in the pork roasting dish with the juice of the remaining orange. Baste the apples and cook for about 45 minutes.

▼

Sweet and Sour Pork

oil for deep frying
1 lb pork fillet, cubed
a little seasoned flour
1 quantity plain Batter (see page 43)
SAUCE:
½ pint water
1 tablespoon vinegar

3 tablespoons Tomato Sauce (see page
  18), or use any sugar-free tomato
  ketchup
1 tablespoon Dietade Fruit Sugar
1 tablespoon sugar-free soy sauce
cornflour to thicken.

Put all the sauce ingredients, except the cornflour, into a pan. Bring to the boil and simmer for 2 minutes. Remove from the heat and allow to cool. Mix the cornflour with a little water. Add to the pan and bring to the boil, stirring all the time. Put to one side.

Heat oil in a deep fryer until smoking. Toss the pork cubes in a little seasoned flour – put into a polythene bag and shake it about a bit. Dip the pork into the batter and fry in the hot oil for about 10 minutes. Drain on kitchen paper. Reheat the sauce and serve hot in a jug or separate dish with the pork.

CLARE'S PORK BOOT

2 lb pork fillet
a little Granose margarine
a little Maison l'Heraud brandy
½ quantity Clare's Pâté (see page 26)

8 oz mushrooms, chopped
7 oz ready-made puff pastry
1 large egg, beaten

Trim all excess fat from the pork fillet. Sauté, to seal, in a little margarine; cool. Paint the surface with brandy and leave to cool. Sauté the mushrooms in margarine.

Roll out the pastry to the length of the pork and to at least twice the width, making sure that there will be enough to completely cover the girth of the pork plus the pâté and mushrooms and leaving sufficient pastry to decorate. Spread some pâté down the centre of the pastry, place the cooled pork fillet on the pâté and spread the remaining pâté over the meat. Place the mushrooms down the centre of the pork fillet and paint the edges of the pastry with beaten egg. Carefully draw up the pastry, enclosing the pork. Pinch the edges tight and leave to cool in the fridge for about 30 minutes.

Remove the "boot" from the fridge, pinch the edges together again and decorate the top with pastry shapes. Pop into a hot oven, 220°C/425°F/Gas 7, for 20 minutes or until the pastry is rising well and starting to turn golden. Lower the temperature to 180°C/350°F/Gas 4 and remove the "boot" from the oven. Brush the surface with beaten egg, then return to the oven for a further 35 minutes.

▲

SPARE RIBS WITH BAR-B-Q SAUCE

2 lb spare ribs or use belly pork slices, sliced into 3 inch lengths
1 quantity Bar-B-Q Sauce (see page 18) plus extra if preferred
MARINADE:
3 tablespoons Tomato Sauce (see page 18), or sugar-free tomato ketchup

2 tablespoons oil
2 tablespoons white wine vinegar
2 tablespoons sugar-free soy sauce
2 garlic cloves, crushed

Mix all the marinade ingredients together. Put the spare ribs in the marinade and leave for at least 5 hours.

Barbecue or cook under a hot grill until crisp and crunchy. Or you can put the ribs in a roasting tin and cook in a warm oven, 160°C/325°F/Gas 3, for about 45 minutes, which makes the meat very tender; then cook under the grill to crispen. Serve with Bar-B-Q sauce.

Top Okra Mixed Vegetables (page 67); *below left* Leek and Potato Pancakes (page 62); *below right* Vegetables in Toast Tartlets (page 66).

CHAPTER FIVE

VEGETABLES

◀

Sugared Carrots

1 bunch young carrots, sliced
water to cover – for each pint add:
½ teaspoon salt

2 teaspoons Dietade Fruit Sugar
2 tablespoons Granose margarine

Put the carrots into a pan and cover with the water. Add the salt, fructose and maragarine. Bring to the boil. Put a lid on and simmer until almost all the liquid has evaporate, shaking the pan occasionally to prevent burning.

▶

Broad Beans with Herb Sauce

2 lb broad beans, shelled
salt and pepper
½ pint Parsley Sauce (see page 15)

1 tablespoon chopped summer
  savoury
3 tablespoons fresh breadcrumbs

Cook the broad beans in salted boiling water for about 5 minutes. Prepare the sauce. Add the savoury and season to taste. Drain the broad beans and put into a fairly shallow ovenproof dish. Pour over the herb sauce and sprinkle the breadcrumbs on the top.

   Bake under the grill, or in a moderate oven, 180°C/350°F/Gas 4, for 15 minutes or until brown on top.

CAULIFLOWER FRITTERS

1½ quantities (¾ pint) Béchamel
  Sauce (see page 14)
1 large egg
1 cauliflower, cut into florets
  discarding stalks

fresh breadcrumbs
fat for deep frying

Prepare the béchamel sauce and allow to cool for 10 minutes, then add the egg.

Cook the cauliflower in boiling salted water for about 3 minutes, drain well.

Turn the béchamel sauce on to a plate. Dip the florets into the sauce to coat well and then dip them into the breadcrumbs. Leave to stand in the fridge for about 30 minutes. Deep fry until golden.

◄

LEEK AND POTATO PANCAKES

1 lb leeks, sliced
1½ lb potatoes, cooked and mashed
5 oz Granose margarine
2 large eggs

salt and pepper
a little flour
8 oz fresh breadcrumbs or wheatgerm
oil for frying

Blanch the leeks in boiling water for 5 minutes. Drain very well and add to the mashed potatoes. Stir well and add the eggs. Season with salt and pepper. Allow to cool.

Turn out onto a floured surface, and roll into a long sausage shape about 2–3 inches across. Cut into 1 inch slices and form into balls. Pop them into the freezer or ice-making compartment of the fridge for about 30 minutes.

Remove from the freezer, flatten and coat with breadcrumbs or wheatgerm. Shallow fry in oil until golden brown.

Variations

Potato Pancakes For plain pancakes leave out the leeks and proceed as before.

▲

"Cookery is become an art, a noble science".
Robert Burton (1577 – 1640)

BOSTON BAKED BEANS

1 lb haricot beans, washed and soaked
  overnight in cold water
8 oz sliced belly pork, derinded and
  chopped
1 teaspoon salt

2 teaspoons Dietade Fruit Sugar
1 teaspoon mustard powder
3 tablespoons Tomato Sauce (see page
  18) plus extra if liked, or use any
  sugar-free tomato ketchup

Drain the beans and cover with fresh water. Bring to the boil and simmer slowly for about 30 minutes until almost tender, then drain.

Put the beans and all the other ingredients into an ovenproof dish with sufficient boiling water to cover. Put on the lid and cook in a cool oven, 140°C/275°F/Gas1, for 2–3 hours. You may need to top up the dish with water occasionally to prevent it from drying out.

Add extra tomato sauce at the end if you prefer a stronger flavour.

◀

BAKED FENNEL

2 bulbs of fennel, sliced crossways
boiling water to cover
1 sugar-free chicken stock cube
2 oz Granose margarine

2 tablespoons plain flour
some finely chopped fresh parsley
a little salt

Put the fennel in a pan, cover with boiling water and add stock cube. Simmer for 10 minutes or until just tender.

Melt the margarine in a separate pan and add the flour. Slowly add ½ of the cooking liquid beating all the time. Bring to the boil, simmer for 2 minutes and add the parsley and salt.

Put the drained fennel into an ovenproof dish and pour over the sauce. Cook in a moderate oven, 190°C/375°F/Gas 5, for about 20 minutes.

◀

*Liza cooked Artichokes for a romantic evening with a
boyfriend, many years ago, and threw the leaves down the
waste disposal. The rest of the evening was spent unblocking
the plumbing with a coat hanger!*

CONTINENTAL POTATO PANCAKES

1 lb potatoes, diced
1 onion, chopped
2 large eggs
salt and pepper

a little sage
a little Granose margarine
a sprinkling of flour

Put all the ingredients except the margarine and flour into a blender and blend for 30 seconds until smooth. Melt a little margarine in a frying pan. Fry tablespoons of the potato mixture, sprinkled with flour, for 5 minutes each side.

▶

GRANDFATHER'S ARTICHOKES IN WINE

3 oz Granose margarine
10 Jerusalem artichokes, sliced
1 parsnip, sliced
3 tomatoes, skinned and sliced

2 fl oz very dry red wine
4 oz mushrooms, sliced
salt and pepper

Melt the margarine and gently fry the artichokes. Add the parsnip and cook for a further 5 minutes. Add the tomatoes, wine, mushrooms and seasoning. Cook gently until all the vegetables are tender.

◀

BRANDIED MUSHROOMS

4 oz green bacon rashers
1½ oz Granose margarine
8 oz mushrooms, sliced

2 tablespoons Maison l'Heraud
    brandy
salt and pepper
chopped freshly parsley

Fry the bacon until crisp, break into small pieces, and set aside.

Heat the margarine in the frying pan, add the mushrooms, coat well and put on the lid. After 5 minutes remove the lid, add the brandy and season with salt and pepper. Replace the lid and cook to desired consistency.

Add the bacon and parsley. Serve with French bread or thick slices of toast.

HOT CAULIFLOWER MAYONNAISE

1 cauliflower, cut into florets
2 oz spring onions, chopped
3 oz Granose margarine

⅓ quantity (⅓ pint) Mayonnaise (see page 17)
a little paprika

Cook the cauliflower in salted boiling water for about 5 minutes until just tender. Meanwhile sauté the onions in the melted margarine until transparent. Remove the onions and put into a shallow ovenproof dish. Drain the cauliflower and arrange on top of the onions with the stalks pointing to the outside. Pour the mayonnaise over the cauliflower, sprinkle over the paprika and bake in a fairly hot oven, 190°C/375°F/ Gas 5, for about 20 minutes.

▲

POTATOES ANNA

2 lb potatoes, thinly sliced
Granose margarine

salt and pepper

Dry the potato slices well. Arrange a layer of potatoes in an ovenproof dish, dot with small pieces of margarine and season with salt and pepper. Continue the layers finishing with margarine and seasoning. Cook in a fairly hot oven 200°C/400°F/Gas 6 for about 20–35 minutes.

Variations

Onion Potatoes Add sautéed onions or garlic between the layers of potato.

Mushroom Potatoes Add sautéed mushrooms between the layers.

Herby Potatoes Add chopped fresh herbs to personal preference.

Anchovy Potatoes Add a scattering of chopped anchovies.

VEGETABLES IN TOAST TARTLETS

4 oz Granose margarine, plus extra to sauté
1 garlic clove, crushed
1 small sliced loaf of bread

small vegetables of choice, such as peas, sweetcorn, mushrooms, baby carrots
1 quantity Hollandaise Sauce (see page 17), plus extra if desired

Mix the margarine and garlic well. Trim the crusts from the bread and square the slices. Thickly spread the bread with the garlic margarine.

Take a tray of patty pans and put the slices of bread, butter-side down, into the patty pans. Press down carefully into the shapes. Leave in the fridge for about 30 minutes until really cold and firm. Put into a fairly hot oven, 200°C/400°F/Gas 6, for 10 minutes or until the bread is golden. Remove from the oven and cool.

Fill the tartlets with sautéed vegetables coated in the Hollandaise sauce.

▼

BRUSSELS SPROUTS WITH CHESTNUTS

1 lb chestnuts
sugar-free chicken stock to cover
1 stick of celery
1 teaspoon Dietade Fruit Sugar

2 oz Granose margarine
2 lb Brussels sprouts
salt and pepper
½ lemon

Score the chestnuts, put into a pan, cover with cold water and bring to the boil. Remove the chestnuts one at a time and peel. If the inner peel dosen't come off easily pop back into the hot water.

Put the nuts into a clean pan and cover with stock. Add the celery and fructose. Bring to the boil and simmer gently for about 35 minutes until the nuts are cooked. Meanwhile cook the sprouts in salted water with the ½ lemon for about 10 minutes. Drain the sprouts and discard the lemon. Drain the nuts.

Melt the margarine in a pan, add the nuts and the sprouts. Shake gently for a couple of minutes. Season with pepper.

OLD ENGLISH PEAS

2 oz Granose margarine
3 good sprigs of mint
1½ lb fresh or frozen peas

1 level teaspoon salt
1 teaspoon Dietade Fruit Sugar

Melt the margarine in a large pan, add the mint and pour in the peas. Sprinkle over the salt and fructose. Put on a lid and cook over a low heat for about 10 minutes, shaking frequently.

▶

COURGETTES WITH TOMATO AND ONION

2 oz Granose margararine
1 garlic clove, crushed
1 onion, sliced lenghtways
4 large courgettes, sliced
2 tomatoes, skinned and deseeded

1 teaspoon finely chopped fresh
   parsley
1 teaspoon finely chopped fresh sage
salt and pepper

Melt the margarine, add the garlic and onion and sauté for about 2 minutes. Add the sliced courgettes and cook until they are tender. Add the other ingredients, stir well and serve hot.

▶

OKRA MIXED VEGETABLES

1 green back bacon rasher
1 onion, chopped
1 green pepper, chopped
18 okra pods, topped, tailed and sliced

3 tomatoes, skinned, deseeded and
   sliced
4 oz sweetcorn kernels
salt and pepper

Fry the bacon until crisp, then crumble and set aside. Fry the onion and green pepper. Add the okra and tomatoes and simmer, stirring occasionally, until most of the moisture has evaporated. Add the bacon and sweetcorn. Season with salt and pepper and serve hot.

Fruit in a Basket (page 79), Croquembouche (page 72).

CHAPTER SIX

PUDDINGS

▲

NUT MOCK CREAM

4 oz raw cashew nuts
1 tablespoon Date Syrup (see page 23)

about 6 tablespoons water
2 oz creamed coconut

Put all the ingredients into a blender and blend to a smooth paste.

Note Use instead of cream on fruit pies or with any pudding. It is wonderful with fruit crumble.

▼

STRAWBERRY CREAM PIE

1 quantity Tart Pastry (see page 83)
1 quantity warm Crème Pâtissière (see page 85)
8 oz hulled strawberries

4 oz sugar-free strawberry jam
2 tablespoons sugar-free apple concentrate

Line an 8 inch flan tin with the pastry, prick the base, line with greaseproof paper and baking beans. Bake blind in a fairly hot oven, 200°C/400°F/Gas 6, for 15 minutes, then remove the paper and beans.

Make the crème pâtissière and while still warm pour into the pastry case. Leave until quite cold.

Cut the strawberries in half and arrange in a pretty pattern on the crème pâtissière cut-side down.

Put the strawberry jam into a pan with the apple concentrate and stir well over a low heat. Put through a sieve and when cool pour gently over the strawberries.

BASIC ICE CREAM

4 large eggs
about 3 dessertspoons Dietade Fruit
  Sugar

½ pint sugar-free soya milk
3 teaspoons pure vanilla essence
6 oz sunflower oil

Separate two of the eggs. Add the fructose to the two yolks and mix together well. Bring the soya milk to the boil and pour on to the yolk and fructose mixture, stirring all the time. Add 1 teaspoon vanilla essence. Put in a container in the freezer for several hours, until set to a mousse-like consistency.

Separate the remaining two eggs, beat the yolks and remaining vanilla essence together until they become light and creamy. Slowly add the sunflower oil, almost a drop at a time, as when making mayonnaise. The oil must be added slowly to the egg yolks to create a thick cream. (Don't taste the mixture now or it may put you off the whole idea!)

When the soya milk mixture has reached its mousse-like consistency, remove from the freezer and give it a good stir. Whip the four egg whites very stiffly indeed. Add the oil cream, then the milk mixture, folding in with a balloon whisk. Now taste the mixture and add more fructose if desired. Return to the freezer and freeze for at least 12 hours.

Variations

Brown Bread Ice Cream Add 6 oz dry brown breadcrumbs to the basic mixture.

Coffee Maple Ice Cream Add 2 dessertspoons instant coffee powder to the boiling soya milk in the basic mixture. Add 2 teaspoons maple flavouring and 1 dessertspoon maple syrup at the end of the recipe.

Walnut and Brandy Ice Cream Add 2 tablespoons Maison l'Heraud brandy to the soya milk in the basic mixture. Add 4 tablespoons finely chopped walnuts at the end of the recipe.

Hazelnut and Chocolate Ice Cream Make 1 quantity Chocolate Topping (see page 85) and leave until firm, then grate it and add with 3 tablespoons chopped hazelnuts to the basic mixture at the end of the recipe.

Raspberry Ice Cream Add 8 oz raspberries or more to taste, to the basic mixture at the end of the recipe.

▶

We tried to make Soya Milk Yoghurt so we could invent Soya Milk Cheese, but the result was disgusting – the only one who liked it was Gertie the Golden Retriever. Ann's Labradors wouldn't even look at it.

BRANDY BUTTER

2 tablespoons Maison l'Heraud
  brandy or ½ teaspoon brandy
  essence

3 oz Dietade Fruit Sugar
8 oz Granose margarine

Warm the brandy gently, add the fructose and stir until dissolved. Allow to cool. Cream the margarine and add the brandy a little at a time. Cream well, put into a serving dish and leave in the fridge until needed.

◄

BREAD AND BUTTER PUDDING

2 oz sultanas
2 oz currants
a little Granose margarine, to spread
4 slices of bread, crusts removed
2 large eggs

1 oz Dietade Fruit Sugar plus a little,
  to sprinkle
¼ pint soya milk
¼ pint water
2 teaspoons pure vanilla essence
a little grated nutmeg

Grease a fairly shallow ovenproof dish, scatter the fruit over the bottom, spread the margarine on each slice of bread and cut each slice into four triangles. Place the slices of bread in a pattern on the top of the fruit.

In a bowl beat the eggs, add the fructose, soya milk, water and vanilla essence. Mix well. Pour over the bread and, with the back of a spoon lightly press the bread down to ensure absorption of the milk mixture.

Sprinkle over a little grated nutmeg. Leave to stand for 1 hour.

Just before the pudding goes in the oven, sprinkle a little fructose over the top.

Bake in a moderate oven, 180°C, 350°F/Gas 4, for 1 hour.

◄

Liza's mother, Clare, said, "Don't ever let tofu pass my lips, or soya milk". So Ann rang up and said that she had made Bread and Butter Pudding, Clare's favourite. Ann drove round with it, Clare demolished the lot and then was told the ingredients and felt sick.

CROQUEMBOUCHE

double quantity Choux Pastry (see page 83)

double quantity Cream Filling (see page 84)

Angel Hair (spun toffee):
8 oz Dietade Fruit Sugar
2 tablespoons boiling water

Pipe the choux mixture on to a baking sheet in small rounds, spacing them well apart. Bake in a very hot oven, 230°C/450°F/Gas 8, for about 15 minutes. Allow to cool. Fill each choux bun with cream filling.

To make the toffee, put the fructose and water into a large pan. Stir over a low heat until the fructose is dissolved, then turn up the heat and cook until it starts to turn golden. Remove the pan from the heat and wait for a few moments for the colour to develop. Return to the heat until a uniform golden colour is achieved, then remove.

On a serving dish make a ring of choux buns, dipping the sides in the melted fructose to stick them together. For the second ring of choux buns, dip the bases in the fructose and stick them on top of the first ring. Continue upwards to make a pyramid and bring to a point at the top. If the fructose is starting to set too firmly, return the pan to a gentle heat.

Next create the effect of spun toffee or Angel Hair around the pyramid. To do this, the fructose must have cooled sufficiently so that when a fork is dipped in and lifted up a fine strand will remain and harden – then you are ready, okay! Dip the fork into the melted fructose and go round and round the pyramid making the strands, dipping the fork in again and again.

Note This is a wonderful, impressive pudding but don't prepare it too far in advance as it collapses fairly quickly. Angel Hair very quickly picks up the moisture from the atmosphere so if it's a damp day, either don't make it at all but simply serve the choux buns with Chocolate Topping (see page 85) or keep the hair dryer handy and give the pyramid a cool gentle blast (not so hard as to dismantle the whole thing) to keep it dry.

◀

*The day we discovered that fructose made toffee and therefore
Angel Hair we danced round the kitchen, cannoning with
Ann's husband Roy who had just returned from work.
We also discovered that we could 'pull' the fructose toffee and
we made some flowers, which Ann knocked on to the floor in
excitement; they shattered like glass and the dogs thought that
it was Christmas.*

CHOCOLATE BRANDIED PEARS

¼ pint sugar-free apple juice
  concentrate
½ pint water
1 strip of orange rind
2 inch cinnamon stick
2 cloves

4 large pears, peeled
double quantity Chocolate Topping
  (see page 85)
2 tablespoons Maison l'Heraud
  brandy

Put the apple concentrate, water, orange rind, cinnamon stick and cloves into a pan. Bring to the boil and simmer for 2 minutes.

Use a melon baller to remove the cores from the bases of the fruit, if liked. Trim the bases from the pears so that they stand up. Stand the pears in the pan and baste well with the liquid. Poach gently, with the lid on, basting frequently, until pears are just tender. Remove the pears from the liquid, drain and put into the fridge to become quite cold.

Remove the cinnamon stick, cloves and orange rind from the liquid and reduce the liquid over a fairly high heat until about 6 tablespoons remain. Leave to cool.

Make the chocolate topping. When the pears are quite cold, blot with kitchen paper until quite dry. Carefully coat each pear with the chocolate topping and return to the fridge until ready to serve.

Stand each pear in an individual glass dish. Add the brandy to the reduced liquid and pour a little around the base of each pear.

◄

MANGO AND LIME MOUSSE

2 teaspoons gelatine
3 teaspoons water
1 large mango, peeled and sliced

juice of 1 lime
Dietade Fruit Sugar to taste
2 large eggs, separated

Sprinkle the gelatine on to the water in a heatproof bowl and leave to become spongy. Stand the bowl in a pan of boiling water until the gelatine has dissolved.

Blend the mango with the lime juice until smooth; add the fructose, egg yolks and gelatine. Blend until smooth, then put into the fridge until almost set.

Whisk the egg whites until very stiff and fold in the fruit mixture. Pour into serving dishes and refrigerate.

ORANGE AND LEMON MERINGUE PIE

1 quantity Tart Pastry (see page 83)
rind and juice of 1 lemon
½ pint fresh orange juice
about 1 dessertspoon Dietade Fruit
   Sugar
2 tablespoons cornflour

4 oz fluid water
3 egg yolks
For the Meringue:
3 egg whites
1 dessertspoon Dietade Fruit Sugar
1 teaspoon cornflour

Line an 8 inch flan tin with the pastry and bake blind in a fairly hot oven, 200°C/400°F/Gas 6, for 15 minutes.

Put the rind and juice of the lemon and the orange juice into a pan with 1 dessertspoon Dietade Fruit Sugar, bring to the boil and simmer for 2 minutes. Mix the 2 tablespoons cornflour with the 4 fl oz water, add three egg yolks and mix well. Allow the orange mixture to cool for about 10 minutes, then slowly add the cornflour mixture, stirring vigorously. Return the pan to the heat and bring to the boil, stirring all the time. Simmer for 1 minute and check for sweetness, adding more fructose if necessary. Pour into the pastry case and leave to cool for about 15 minutes.

For the meringue, whisk the egg whites until very stiff, fold in the 1 dessertspoon Dietade Fruit Sugar and the 1 teaspoon cornflour. Pipe on to the orange and lemon mixture. Pop into a fairly hot oven, 190°C/375°F/Gas 5, for about 10 minutes or until the peaks are golden.

▲

SPOTTED DICK

8 oz plain flour, sifted
1 teaspoon baking powder
½ teaspoon cinnamon
½ teaspoon nutmeg
a pinch of salt

4 oz suet, finely chopped
6 oz mixed raisins, currants and
   sultanas
cold water to mix the dough

Mix the flour, baking powder, spices and salt. Add the suet and the mixed dried fruit. Make into a dough, adding a little cold water.

Put into a greased basin, cover with greaseproof paper and foil. Boil in a pan for 2½ hours.

Serve with 1 quantity hot Crème Pâtissière (see page 85) adding some extra pure vanilla essence – and for a special party add 1 tablespoon Maison l'Heraud brandy.

CHRISTMAS PUDDING

Makes two puddings (in 2 pint size basins) or make one large round pudding
   in calico cloth

4 oz flour
½ teaspoon salt
8 oz fine white breadcrumbs
8 oz shredded suet
8 oz raisins
8 oz sultanas
12 oz currants
8 oz minced dates
4 oz chopped dried pears
4 oz chopped dried peaches
4 oz chopped dried figs
4 oz chopped candied peel (see page
   86)
1 apple, grated
1 carrot, grated
2 oz chopped almonds

3 oz maple syrup
3 tablespoons Date Syrup (see page
   23)
3 tablespoons sugar-free apple juice
   concentrate
rind and juice of 1 lemon plus extra
   juice if necessary
rind and juice of 1 orange plus extra
   juice if necessary
3 teaspoons mixed spice
2 teaspoons grated nutmeg
3 large eggs
2 tablespoons Maison l'Heraud
   brandy or 2 teaspoons brandy
   essence
silver pudding favours

Mix all the ingredients (except the brandy and silver favours) together in a bowl. Cover with a clean tea towel and leave to stand for 24 hours. At the end of that time you may have to add a little more fruit juice if the mixture is too stiff. Pour into two 2 pint pudding basins, cover with greaseproof paper and foil, tie with string, and steam for 6 hours. Store in the freezer when cold.

   If you want the traditional round-shaped pudding take one 25 inch square of calico cloth, drape across a bowl, pour on boiling water and wring out well. Spread the cloth out on a flat surface and sprinkle liberally with plain flour. Carefully drape the cloth over a large pudding basin and tip the pudding mixture in, firming it down. Drawing in the sides of the cloth and leaving a gap to allow for expansion, tie the top with string. Leave enough string to hang the pudding up and to lift it in and out of the pan. Lift the pudding and lower into boiling water in a very large pan, such as a preserving pan, so that the pudding floats in the water. Boil for 6 hours with the lid on. At no time allow the water to go off the boil and always keep the pan topped up with boiling water. Remove the pudding from the water and hang it up to cool. Freeze until Christmas.

   On Christmas Day boil the thawed pudding for 2 hours. Turn on to serving dish and poke in the silver favours. With the back of a spoon, make an indentation in the top and pour the brandy in the hollow. Put holly around the plate. Carefully set fire to the brandy and serve with Brandy Butter.

TRIFLE

1 Fatless Sponge (see page 81)
4 oz sugar-free jam
3 level teaspoons gelatine
1 pint of sugar-free fruit juice
2 tablespoons Maison l'Heraud
    brandy

8 oz fresh fruit or canned and drained
    sugar-free fruit of choice
1½ quantities Crème Pâtissière (see
    page 85)
1 quantity Cream Filling (see page 85)
toasted almonds

Split the sponge in two, fill with jam and then cut into pieces and put into a serving dish.

Dissolve the gelatine in ¼ pint of the fruit juice in a heatproof bowl and stand the bowl in a pan of hot water until it becomes clear. Mix with the remaining fruit juice.

Sprinkle the brandy on the sponge and sprinkle over the fruit. Pour over the gelatine fruit juice. Leave to set.

Make the crème pâtissière and allow to cool, but stir frequently while cooling so that a skin does not form. Pour over the cake and jelly. Pipe the cream filling on the top and decorate with the toasted almonds.

▶

FRUIT FRITTERS

8 oz flour, sifted
½ teaspoon salt
2 tablespoons Granose margarine,
    melted
about ½ pint water

1 tablespoon Maison l'Heraud brandy
    (or few drops of brandy essence)
2 egg whites, stiffly beaten
selected fruits of choice (see **Note**)
oil for frying

Into a large bowl put the flour, salt and melted margarine. Mix into a batter with the water and brandy. Just before using, fold in the egg whites.

Dip the fruits of your choice in the batter and fry in very hot oil. Drain on kitchen paper.

Note Many different fruits make delicious fritters: use rings of peeled and cored apples, fresh and non-soak dried apricots, cherries with stalks to hold by, destoned fresh dates or figs filled with very thick Crème Pâtissière (see page 85) flavoured with a little brandy, fresh pineapple pieces, or peach slices.

Flower fritters are interesting – dip elder flowers or violets or marrow blossoms or nasturtiums in the batter and fry.

Mix some chestnut purée with some sugar-free apricot jam to a stiff paste and form into small balls; put into a freezer for 30 minutes to firm, then dip in the batter and fry.

SWEET PANCAKES

a little oil for frying
Plain Pancake Batter:
4 oz plain flour
2 large eggs

OR

Rich Pancake Batter:
4 oz plain flour
3 large eggs
2 tablespoons Maison l'Heraud
   brandy

a pinch of salt
pancake filling of choice
about ½ pint water (to make a creamy
   consistency)

1 tablespoon Dietade Fruit Sugar
sufficient water to make a cream-like
   consistency

To make either the plain or the rich batter, put the flour (and salt if using) into a basin and add the eggs with some of the water. Beat very well until all lumps are removed. Add sufficient liquid to make a cream–like consistency.

To cook the pancakes, heat a little oil in a frying pan and pour in batter to thinly coat the base of the pan. Cook for a few minutes, then lift an edge to see if the bottom is turning brown. If so, toss the pancake and cook the other side. Transfer to a plate and keep warm.

Repeat with the remaining batter, stacking the cooked pancakes with greaseproof paper between each. Prepare a filling, roll and serve.

Pancake Fillings

Hazelnut Fillings Cream 6 oz Granose margarine. Stir in 3 oz roasted chopped hazelnuts, 1 tablespoon grated orange rind, 2 tablespoons fresh orange juice, 1 tablespoon Maison l'Heraud brandy and 1 tablespoon Dietade Fruit Sugar. Spread a little filling on each pancake and roll up. Put in a heatproof dish in a fairly hot oven, 200°C/400°F/ Gas 6, for 10 minutes.

Strawberry Filling Put 2 oz Granose margarine, 1 tablespoon Dietade Fruit Sugar, 3 oz fresh orange juice and 1 tablespoon Maison l'Heraud brandy in a pan and bring slowly to the boil. Boil slowly for 5 minutes, stirring all the time. Remove from the heat and allow to cool for 15 minutes. Fold in 1 punnet hulled and sliced strawberries. Using a slotted spoon, divide the strawberries between the pancakes and roll them up. Reboil the liquid, pour over the pancakes and serve at once.

Pineapple Filling Follow the recipe for strawberry filling but use 3 slices fresh pineapple instead of the strawberries.

Noel Pancakes Mix 3 tablespoons Mincemeat (see page 115) with 1 quantity Crème Pâtissière (see page 85). Put a little filling on each pancake, roll up and put in a fairly hot oven, 190°C/375°F/Gas 5, for 10 minutes. Just before serving throw on some Maison l'Heraud brandy and set fire to it.

TOFFEE CREAM PIE

1 quantity Tart Pastry (see page 83)
3 large eggs, separated
2 oz Dietade Fruit Sugar
3 teaspoons gelatine
3 tablespoons water
1 tablespoon Maison l'Heraud brandy
   (optional)

1 teaspoon maple flavouring
1 quantity Cream Filling (see page 84)
For the Toffee:
3 oz Dietade Fruit Sugar
1 teaspoon water

Line a pie dish with the pastry and bake blind in a fairly hot oven, 200°C/400°F/Gas 6, for 15 minutes.

Put the toffee ingredients into a pan and stir over a low heat until the fructose has dissolved. Turn the heat up, without stirring, and when the mixture turns golden brown remove the pan from the heat.

Put the egg yolks in a heatproof bowl and beat with the 2 oz Dietade Fruit Sugar over a pan of simmering water. Beat until the mixture becomes light and creamy. Continue beating at high speed and trickle in the toffee mixture.

Sprinkle the gelatine over the 3 tablespoons of water in a heatproof bowl and leave until spongy, then stand the bowl in a pan of boiling water until the gelatine has dissolved. Add to the toffee mixture with the brandy and maple flavouring. Whip the egg whites until very stiff and fold in.

Pour into the pastry case and leave until set. Decorate the top with the cream filling.

▶

JAM ROLY POLY

8 oz plain flour
1 teaspoon baking powder
4 oz suet, finely chopped
a pinch of salt

1 dessertspoon Dietade Fruit Sugar
cold water to mix the dough
8 oz sugar-free jam

Mix the flour, baking powder and suet. Add the salt and fructose. Make a firm dough, adding the necessary water. On a floured surface roll out the dough to a rectangle about ¼ inch thick. Spread the jam all over and then roll up, Swiss roll fashion, pinching both ends. Put on to a clean floured piece of linen or double muslin. Tie both ends, Christmas cracker style. Put into a pan of boiling water and boil for 2½ hours.

Serve hot with more jam heated and poured over and with hot Crème Pâtissière (see page 85) flavoured with extra pure vanilla essence.

FRUIT IN A BASKET

Makes 8–10 baskets

Brandy Snap Baskets:
2 oz Granose magarine
1 oz Dietade Fruit Sugar
4 tablespoons maple syrup
¼ teaspoon cream of tartar
Filling:
a selection of fruit such as mango and kiwi fruit, or lychees and pineapple
Cream Filling (see page 85) optional, a little Angel Hair (see page 85)

¼ teaspoon bicarbonate of soda
1 teaspoon ginger
2 oz plain flour

To make the brandy snap mixture, put the margarine, fructose and maple syrup into a pan and stir over a low heat until well blended. Add all the other ingredients and stir well. Grease a baking tray and put teaspoons of mixture on to the tray; allow plenty of space between them as they will spread. Bake in a fairly hot oven, 190°C/375°F/Gas 5, for about 5 minutes until lightly golden.

To shape the baskets, allow the brandy snap mixture to cool slightly, then carefully lift each round off the tray and gently shape over a small upturned bowl. If the rounds become too firm, pop them back into the oven for a few moments to soften. The baskets will harden very quickly; lift gently from the bowl and put on one side to cool completely.

For the filling, chop up a selection of fruit to your choice and fill each basket. Top each with a dollop of cream filling if desired. Just before serving spin a little angel hair for each basket and set on the top.

▶

RICE PUDDING

1 pint soya milk
2 oz pudding rice
1½ oz Dietade Fruit Sugar

2 oz Granose margarine
2 teaspoons pure vanilla essence
¼ teaspoon grated nutmeg

Put all the ingredients into a saucepan, bring to the boil and simmer for 5 minutes. Remove the pan to a work surface away from the source of heat.

Wrap the pan carefully in a large towel or blanket to conserve the heat. Look at it after 2 hours; if it isn't thick enough give it a good stir and bring it back to the boil, simmer for 5 minutes, wrap up again in the towel or blanket, and leave for 2 further hours.

Note This is Ann's own Fuel Economy Method of cooking rice pud.

Back Cinnamon Torte (page 90); *front* Apricot and Brandy Gateau (page 88).
Assorted sweets: Marzipan Dates (page 95), Chocolate (page 95), Apricot and Almond Truffles (page 97).

CHAPTER SEVEN

GATEAUX, CAKES, BISCUITS AND SWEETS

▲

BASIC SPONGE

4 oz Dietade Fruit Sugar
4 oz Granose margarine

2 large eggs, separated
4 oz sponge flour

Cream the fructose and margarine together until light and creamy, then add the yolks one at a time. Fold in the flour and lastly the stiffly whipped egg whites.

Bake in an 8 inch round sponge tin in a moderate oven, 180°C/350°F/Gas 4, for 35 minutes.

▶

FATLESS SPONGE

4 large eggs
3 oz Dietade Fruit Sugar

4 oz sponge flour

Put the eggs into very warm water for 10 minutes – it makes them whip better. Remove from the water and separate. Cream the yolks until light and fluffy, then add half the fructose. Whisk the whites until very stiff. Fold the remaining fructose into the whites.

Fold the whites alternately with the flour into the yolk mixture using a balloon whisk.

Bake in a greased and lined 8 inch tin in a moderate oven, 180°C/350°F/Gas 4, for 30 minutes.

BASIC SWEET SHORTCRUST PASTRY

3 oz Granose margarine
2 oz sugar-free cooking fat such as
  Trex
8 oz plain flour

1 dessertspoon Dietade Fruit Sugar
2 tablespoons cold water

Rub the fats into the flour and fructose, until like breadcrumbs. Bring together to a dough-like consistency with the water. Leave to stand in a cool place for 30 minutes before using.

Variation

Savoury Shortcrust Pastry Follow the basic sweet shortcrust pastry recipe but omit the fructose and substitute 1 teaspoon salt.

◄

SHORTBREAD PASTRY

5 oz Granose margarine
9 oz plain flour, sifted
2 oz Dietade Fruit Sugar

1 oz ground almonds
1 large egg
a few drops of pure vanilla essence

Rub the margarine into the flour. Add the fructose, ground almonds, egg and vanilla. Work into a ball, then leave in a cold place for 1 hour.

Variations

Shortbread Pastry II

6 oz Granose margarine
2 oz Dietade Fruit Sugar
2 large eggs

12 oz plain flour, sifted
2 oz ground rice
½ teaspoon baking powder

Cream the margarine and fructose. Add the eggs, one at a time, beating well after each addition. Add the flour, ground rice and baking powder. Knead the creamed mixture to form a ball. Refrigerate for 45 minutes before use.

Shortbread Biscuits To make the biscuits, simply roll out the basic pastry and cut into fingers. Place on a greased baking sheet and bake in a cool oven, 140°C/275°F/Gas 1, for 50 minutes.

TART PASTRY

4 oz Granose margarine
8 oz plain flour
1 tablespoon Dietade Fruit Sugar

1 large egg
a pinch of salt
about 2 tablespoons cold water

Rub the fat into the flour. Add the fructose and stir in the egg and salt. Add sufficient water to form a ball. Leave in the fridge for a least 1 hour before use.

▶

ALMOND PASTRY

6 oz Granose margarine
1 oz Dietade Fruit Sugar
1 oz ground almonds

8 oz plain flour
1½ tablespoons water

Cream the margarine and fructose together. Add the almonds and flour. Bring together to form a pastry ball with the water. Refrigerate for 30 minutes before using.

◀

CHOUX PASTRY

¼ pint water
1½ oz sugar-free cooking fat such as Trex
3 oz plain flour

2 large eggs, beaten
1 teaspoon baking powder

Put the water and cooking fat in a pan and bring to the boil, making sure that the Trex has completely melted.

Tip the flour on to the fast boiling liquid, stir vigorously and the mixture should come together in a big ball. Cook over a low heat for about 30 seconds, stirring all the time.

At this point, if you have a mixer, tip the flour ball into the mixer bowl. Allow to cool for 5 minutes and slowly add the beaten eggs, beating vigorously all the time. Lastly sprinkle over the baking powder and incorporate very well. Add a little more water, before using, if the mixture feels too stiff and you need to pipe the choux pastry.

RICH PASTRY

7 oz Granose margarine
8 oz plain flour
2 dessertspoons Dietade Fruit sugar

2 teaspoons pure vanilla essence
about 2 tablespoons cold water

Rub the fat into the flour. Add the fructose, vanilla essence and water and work together into a ball. Leave to rest in a cool place for 30 minutes.

▶

BASIC CREAM FILLING

½ pint soya milk
5 heaped teaspoons cornflour
1 large egg, beaten

3 heaped dessertspoons fructose
8 oz Granose margarine
3 teaspoons pure vanilla essence

Bring the soya milk to the boil, then remove from the heat. Mix the cornflour with a little cold water and add to the boiled milk, stirring vigorously all the time. Return to the heat and cook gently until thick, stirring all the time. Remove from the heat and allow to cool for 5 minutes.

Slowly add the beaten egg, stirring vigorously all the time. Return to the heat and bring just to the boil, stirring all the time. Add the fructose and stir well. Pour on to a plate and cover with a sheet of clingfilm (to prevent a skin forming); leave until quite cold.

Cream the margarine and add the cold mixture a tablespoon at a time, beating well with each addition. Add the vanilla essence.

Note This cream filling and the variations freeze very well.

Variations

Coffee Filling Add 1 dessertspoon instant coffee to the soya milk at the beginning of the recipe.

Chocolate Filling Mix 2 dessertspoons cocoa powder to a cream with a little of the soya milk and add to the remaining soya milk at the beginning of the recipe. Bring to the boil, stirring all the time with a balloon whisk.

Orange Filling Add 1 teaspoon finely grated orange rind and 2 dessertspoons sugar-free orange juice concentrate at the end of the recipe.

Almond Filling Add 1 teaspoon almond essence with the pure vanilla essence at the end of the recipe.

CRÈME PÂTISSIÈRE

3 oz Granose margarine
2 tablespoons plain flour
¼ pint soya milk
¼ pint water

1 large egg, separated
1 tablespoon Dietade Fruit Sugar
2 teaspoons pure vanilla essence

Melt the margarine in a pan and add the flour. Mix the water and the milk together. Slowly add to the margarine, stirring all the time as when making a white sauce. Bring to the boil, stirring all the time, and simmer for 2 minutes.

Remove from the heat and allow to cool for 10 minutes.

Add the egg yolk and fructose. Fold in the whipped egg white, return to a very low heat and cook for 1 minute, delicately folding the mixture. Add the vanilla.

Leave until cold before using.

Note Where a very thick crème pâtissière is required simply add less milk and water, then cook for longer.

◀

CHOCOLATE TOPPING

3 teaspoons cocoa powder
4 tablespoons water
about 4 oz creamed coconut, grated

a little Dietade Fruit Sugar or Date
    Syrup (see page 23)

Put the cocoa powder and water together in a pan and bring to the boil. Add the grated coconut and sweeten to taste with fructose or date syrup. Allow to cool to a coating consistency before using.

The chocolate topping can also be put in a small dish in the fridge and left to become very firm. You can then grate it for decoration.

▶

MARZIPAN – I

1½ oz Dietade Fruit Sugar
1 large egg yolk
2 drops pure vanilla essence

2 drops almond essence
4 oz ground almonds

Mix the fructose with the egg yolk and leave for 30 minutes. Mix in the essences and then knead in the ground almonds. Store in the fridge.

MARZIPAN – II

2 oz Granose margarine
4 oz Dietade Fruit Sugar
2 tablespoons water

2 small teaspoons almond essence
4 oz soya flour

Melt the margarine in a pan and add the fructose, water and essence. Stir over a low heat for 1 minute. Remove from the heat and knead in the soya flour.

▶

CANDIED PEEL – I

a pinch of bicarbonate of soda
water

peel from 3 oranges or from a mixture
   of oranges and lemons
6 oz Dietade Fruit Sugar

Dissolve the bicarbonate of soda in a little water, pour over the peel and sufficient boiling water to cover. Leave it to stand for 20 minutes, then rinse and drain several times.

Cover the peel with cold water, bring to the boil and simmer until tender. Drain the peel.

Dissolve the fructose in 4 fl oz water. Add the peel and simmer with the lid off until all the syrup is absorbed and the peel is clear.

Put the peel into an airtight container and it will keep for about 4 weeks. Alternatively, when cold, chop the peel, put on a tray and open freeze; keep in freezer containers.

◀

CANDIED PEEL – II

peel from 3 small oranges
peel from 1 lemon

sugar-free apple juice concentrate, to
   cover

Cut the peel into strips and put in a pan. Cover with water and bring to the boil, then drain. Repeat this boiling and draining process five times until the peel is soft.

Cover the peel with apple juice and cook gently until all the apple juice is absorbed.

Put the strips of peel on to a wire tray and place in a very cool oven, 110°C/225°F/Gas ¼, for about 1 hour. Store in a clean dry jar.

BLACK FOREST GÂTEAU

4 large eggs
3½ oz Dietade Fruit Sugar plus extra
   to taste
1 dessertspoon cocoa powder
4 oz sponge flour
8 oz fresh or frozen cherries or sugar-
   free canned
2 teaspoons cornflour

a little Maison l'Heraud brandy
   (optional)
double quantity of Cream Filling (see
   page 84)
some split and toasted almonds to coat
   sides
1 quantity Chocolate Topping (see
   page 85)

Stand the eggs in very warm water for 10 minutes. Remove from the water and separate. Cream the yolks until creamy, then add half the fructose and beat well. Whisk the whites until stiff. Fold the remaining fructose into the whites.

Into a separate bowl sieve the cocoa powder and flour gradually. Add the flour and egg whites alternately to the egg yolk mixture.

Put into a greased and lined 8 inch tin and bake in a moderate oven, 180°C/350°F/Gas 4, for 30 minutes. Leave to cool.

Simmer the cherries in a little water or fruit juice until soft, then cool and remove the stones. Mix the cornflour with a little water, add to the cherry juice and cook until thick. At this point sweeten to taste with a little fructose. Add the cherries to the sauce and leave to cool.

Split the sponge twice to form three rounds. Spinkle a little brandy on the base sponge. Spread over the cherry mixture. Put another sponge on the top of the cherries and sprinkle with brandy. Spread with some of the cream filling, put the remaining sponge on the top and sprinkle that with brandy.

Into a piping bag with a large star nozzle put enough cream filling to pipe around the top. Spread more cream filling around the sides and sprinkle liberally with almonds. Pipe swirls of cream filling around the top making sure that they touch.

Make the chocolate topping and allow to cool. Pour on to the top of the cake, tilting the plate so that the top of the cake is covered.

▲

*A little boy at Sophie's school hearing that Sophie was allergic
(not accurate but a simple word to use so people will
understand) to milk, thought about it and then said "Please
miss, I'm allergic to beetroot!"*

APRICOT AND BRANDY GÂTEAU

1 Fatless Sponge (see page 81)
1 quantity Brandy Snaps (see Fruit in a Basket page 79)
1 quantity Cream Filling (see page 84)

8 oz can sugar-free apricots or soaked dried apricots

Make the sponge, brandy snaps and cream filling; leave to cool.

Split the cooled sponge in half. Crumble two of the brandy snaps fairly finely with a rolling pin. Spread some of the cream filling over the base sponge and sprinkle over the crushed brandy snaps. Reserve some of the apricots for decoration, chop the remainder and sprinkle over. Put the second sponge on top of the apricots.

Pipe some cream filling into the ends of each brandy snap. Spread the remaining cream over the top of the cake. Arrange the brandy snaps on the top, wheel-fashion and dot a few apricots around too.

Note For this recipe, shape the Brandy Snaps traditionally by rolling the cooling biscuits around a buttered wooden spoon handle; leave to set and then twist off gently and cool.

▶

PINEAPPLE AND KIWI GÂTEAU

1 small fresh ripe pineapple
3 or 4 kiwi fruit
1 Fatless Sponge (see page 81)

double quantity Crème Pâtissière (see page 85) or Cream Filling (see page 85)

Remove the peel from the pineapple and the kiwi fruit. Reserve some pineapple, cut into long strips, and some kiwi fruit, cut into long strips, for decoration. Finely chop up the remaining kiwi fruit and pineapple. Split the sponge into two. Spread half the cream filling on the bottom sponge and sprinkle with the chopped fruit. Put the other sponge on the top and spread with the remaining cream, taking it down the sides. Retain a little cream for piping decoration.

Decorate the top and sides with the strips of fruit, piping the cream between the strips.

GÂTEAU ST. HONORÉ

double quantity Choux Pastry (see page 83)
1 quantity Shortbread Pastry (see page 82)
double quantity Crème Pâtissière (see page 85)

12 oz apricots (fresh and stoned, sugar-free canned, or dried and soaked)
1 tablespoon Maison l'Heraud brandy
4 tablespoons sugar-free apricot jam
4 oz Dietade Fruit Sugar
2 tablespoons boiling water

Prepare the choux pastry and using a plain large duchesse potato size nozzle pipe an 8 inch diameter ring of paste on to a greased baking sheet. Then pipe another ring inside the first ring so they just touch. Bake in a very hot oven, 230°C/450°F/Gas 8, for about 20 minutes or until golden brown. On a separate greased baking sheet pipe small choux balls (the size of large walnuts). Bake these for about 10 minutes or until golden brown. Allow to cool.

Prepare the shortbread pastry and roll out to a circle the same diameter as the baked choux ring. Prick with a fork and bake in a cool oven, 140°C/275°F/Gas 1, for about 50 minutes. Leave to cool.

While the shortbread is baking, prepare the crème pâtissière. Take 4 oz of the apricots and either put them through a sieve or blend until smooth, then add to the crème pâtissière. Slice the choux ring in two and fill with some crème pâtissière. Make small holes in the choux buns and pipe in some crème pâtissière.

Mix the brandy with the apricot jam and spread it over the surface of the cold shortbread. Place the filled choux ring on top.

Put the fructose in a pan, and add the boiling water and stir until all the fructose is dissolved. Over a fairly high heat boil the mixture until it becomes golden (be careful as it colours very quickly and will continue to colour when the pan is removed from the heat for a little while).

Remove the pan from the heat, take the small filled choux buns and dip each one into the toffee. Set the buns side-by-side on the top of the choux ring. Fill the centre with the remaining crème pâtissière, halve the remaining apricots and arrange cut-side down across the top of the crème pâtissière.

By this time the toffee will have started to cool sufficiently so that when you put a fork in and pull it out it will leave a thread and you are ready to make the Angel Hair (spun toffee) (see **Note**). Bringing the pan close to the gateau, dip a fork in the toffee and draw the toffee thread around the outside of the gâteau, dipping the fork in as necessary until all the toffee is used. If the toffee becomes too stiff, return to a very low heat until it softens and the toffee becomes manageable again.

Note It is a good idea to leave the spinning of the Angel Hair until no longer than 1 hour before serving as the toffee absorbs the moisture in the air very easily.

CHESTNUT TORTE

4 large eggs, separated
4 oz Dietade Fruit Sugar
½ teaspoon pure vanilla essence
1 tablespoon Maison l'Heraud brandy
 or 1 teaspoon brandy essence

9 oz can unsweetened chestnut purée
2¼ oz self-raising flour, sifted
1 quantity Cream Filling (see page 84)
8 oz fresh hulled raspberries or
 strawberries

Beat together the egg yolks, fructose and vanilla essence until thick and creamy. Add the brandy and half of the chestnut purée. Lightly fold in the sieved flour and lastly fold in the stiffly beaten egg whites. Pour into two greased and lined 9 inch cake tins. Bake in a moderate oven, 180°C/350°F/Gas 4, for 20–25 minutes. Remove from the oven and cool.

Make the cream filling, adding the remaining chesnut purée. Sandwich the cakes together with some of the cream filling and some of the strawberries, reserving some for decoration. Spread the remaining cream on the top and pipe some round the top edge. Decorate with the remaining strawberries.

▲

CINNAMON TORTE

1 quantity Rich Pastry (see page 84)
2 teaspoons cinnamon
1 quantity Chocolate Topping (see
 page 85)

3 oz ground almonds
1 quantity Cream Filling (see page 84)

Make the pastry, adding the cinnamon to the mixture. Leave to rest in a cool place for 30 minutes. On pieces of greasproof paper, trace around a 7 inch cake tin six times giving six paper rounds. Cut the pastry into six equal pieces, roll out on the papers and trim to the exact shapes. You should now have six rounds of pastry. Bake in a fairly hot oven, 200°C/400°F/Gas 6, for 6–8 minutes. Watch carefully, the pastry should be just pale straw coloured. Leave on the papers to cool.

When the pastry is cool, carefully remove all the greasproof paper. Select the most perfect pastry round, spread with the chocolate topping and quickly sprinkle over a little of the ground almonds before the chocolate dries. Add the remaining ground almonds to the cream filling. Spread the cream filling equally on to the remaining five pastry rounds. Stack them up together and finish with the chocolate coated round.

LARDY CAKE

⅓ quantity (1 lb) White Bread Dough
  (see page 101)
3 oz lard
2 oz sultanas
2 oz raisins

2 oz Dietade Fruit Sugar plus 1
  tablespoon
½ teaspoon mixed spice
½ teaspoon grated nutmeg

Roll out the dough to an oblong. Spread two-thirds of the dough with half of the lard. Sprinkle with half the sultanas, raisins, fructose, mixed spice and nutmeg. As for puff pastry, fold the dough into three from one of the short sides. Give the dough a quarter turn so that the folded edges are now to the sides and roll out again to an oblong. Sprinkle over the remaining half of the ingredients, fold up again, then roll out and shape to fit a greased 7 inch round sponge tin. Lift the dough into the tin and leave to rise with an oiled polythene bag over the top until doubled in size.

    Bake in a hot oven, 220°C/425°F/Gas 7, for 30 minutes; remove from the oven and brush the top with 1 tablespoon fructose dissoved in 1 dessertspoon boiling water, then return to the oven for a further 10 minutes.

▶

SEEDY CAKE (CHOKE CAKE)

6 oz Dietade Fruit Sugar
8 oz Granose margarine
4 large eggs
8 oz plain flour

½ oz caraway seeds
1 dessertspoon Maison l'Heraud
  brandy (optional)

Cream the fructose and margarine together until light and fluffy. Add the eggs one at a time beating well; with each egg add 1 tablespoon of the flour. Fold in the remaining flour and the caraway seeds. Pour into a greased and lined 8 inch round cake tin and bake in a moderate oven, 180°C/350°F/Gas 4, for 1½ hours.

◀

"Then receive as best such an advent comes, with a legion of cooks, and an army of slaves."
Lord Byron

CHRISTMAS CAKE

3 oz minced dates
2 oz chopped dried figs
2 oz chopped dried apple
2 oz chopped dried pear
3 lb mixed raisins, sultanas and
    currants
3 tablespoons Maison l'Heraud
    brandy or sugar-free apple juice
    concentrate plus extra for pouring
8 oz Granose margarine
2 oz Dietade Fruit Sugar
2 teaspoons almond essence
2 heaped teaspoons mixed spice

1 heaped teaspoon grated nutmeg
3 oz creamed coconut mixed with 2
    tablespoons boiling water
6 large eggs
8 oz plain flour
2 oz chopped walnuts
2 oz chopped blanched almonds
2 oz chopped Candied Peel (see page
    86) optional
a little sugar-free apple juice, if needed
sugar-free jam
8 quantities Marzipan (see pages 85
    and 86)

Steep all the fruit in the brandy or apple juice overnight.

Cream the margarine with the fructose until light and fluffy then add the almond essence, spices and coconut. Add the eggs one at a time, beating well after each addition. Fold in the flour, fruit, nuts and peel, adding some apple juice if the mixture is too stiff. Put into a greased 10 inch square or round tin lined with baking paper or a double layer of greaseproof paper; if possible leave to stand overnight before baking.

Bake in a cool oven, 140°C/275°F/Gas 1, for about 3–4 hours. Test with a skewer; if it comes out clean the cake is done.

Pour over a little more brandy or apple juice while the cake is cooling in the tin. Don't attempt to remove the cake from the tin until it is completely cold. Brush the top with jam and cover with marzipan.

▶

MILLE FEUILLES

7 oz ready-made puff pastry
1 quantity Cream Filling (see page 84)

fresh fruit or sugar-free jam

Cut the pastry in half and roll to two oblongs of equal size and about ⅛ inch thick. With a floured knife cut a tiny amount off each edge as this makes the pastry rise more evenly. Put the pastry to rest on a baking sheet in a cool place for 30 minutes.

Bake in a very hot oven, 230°C/450°F/Gas 8, for about 10 minutes; then turn the oven down, to 200°C/400°F/Gas 6, until the pastry is golden brown. Leave to cool.

When cool split each pastry oblong in half and sandwich together with cream filling and fruit or jam. Pipe a little cream filling on to the top and decorate with fruit – wild strawberries are a great favourite.

FRUIT PIE

1 quantity Tart Pastry (see page 83)
8 oz dates
rind and juice of 1 lemon
4 oz sultanas
4 oz raisins
1 oz chopped dried figs

1 oz chopped dried pears
2 oz Granose margarine
2 teaspoons mixed spice
½ pint water
1 tablespoon cornflour
1 tablespoon Maison l'Heraud brandy
or fresh orange juice

Prepare the pastry and leave in the fridge.

Into a pan put all the ingredients except the cornflour and brandy or orange juice. Cook gently over a low heat until the mixture thickens, stirring all the time. Blend the cornflour with the brandy or orange juice, add to the fruit mixture stirring all the time. Return to the heat and stir until the mixture boils. Simmer for 1 minute, then remove from the heat and allow to cool.

Line an 8 inch pie plate with two-thirds of the pastry. Spoon over the cooled fruit filling. Roll out the remaining pastry for the lid, pressing the edges well together. Bake in a fairly hot oven, 200°C/400°F/Gas 6, for 30–35 minutes.

◄

BAKEWELL TART

5 oz Granose margarine
5 oz Dietade Fruit Sugar
3 large eggs
2 oz ground almonds
2 oz cake crumbs from a Basic Sponge
(see page 81) or an extra 2 oz
ground almonds if no cake is
available

1 quantity Almond Pastry (see page
83)
2 tablespoons sugar-free jam of choice
a few slivered almonds

Cream the margarine and fructose together until light and frothy. Beat in the eggs, one at a time. Fold in the ground almonds, cake crumbs and almond essence.

Line an 8 inch pie plate with the pastry; leave enough with the trimmings to make a lattice design on top. Spread the pastry with jam. Pour over the almond mixture. Roll out the remaining pastry, cut into thin strips and place on top of the tart in a lattice pattern. Sprinkle the almonds in between the lattice strips.

Bake in a fairly hot oven, 200°C/400°F/Gas 6, for 20 minutes. Lower the temperature to 180°C/350°F/Gas 4, and bake for a further 15 minutes. Serve hot or cold.

GINGERBREAD

2 oz Granose margarine
5 oz maple syrup
3 oz Dietade Fruit Sugar
1 teaspoon ground ginger
½ teaspoon cinnamon

12 oz plain flour
a pinch of salt
½ teaspoon bicarbonate of soda
1 large egg

Gently heat the margarine, maple syrup, fructose and spices in a pan until the fructose is dissolved. Leave until quite cold.

Sift the flour, salt and bicarbonate of soda into a bowl. Stir well. Add the cooled syrup mixture and the egg, then knead to a smooth dough. Leave to stand for a few hours or overnight.

Roll out the dough to ¼ inch thick and with fancy cutters cut out shapes such as gingerbread men. Place the gingerbread shapes on a baking sheet and bake in a fairly hot oven, 200°C/400°F/Gas 6, for 10–15 minutes.

◄

MACAROONS

3 oz Dietade Fruit Sugar
1 large egg white
1 teaspoon almond essence
2½ oz ground almonds

2 oz ground rice
½ teaspoon baking powder
rice paper
some split almonds

Mix the fructose into the egg white. We gave it a beat with a whisk for good measure. Leave for a while, then add the almond essence. Add the ground almonds, ground rice and baking powder.

Drop teaspoonfuls on to the rice paper in a baking sheet; or if you have no rice paper, then use clear roasting bags. Pop a split almond on the top of each macaroon. Bake in a cool oven, 150°C/300°F/Gas 2, for 15 minutes or until golden.

Variations

Coconut Macaroon Stacks Add about 3 oz desiccated coconut and mould into little domes on the rice paper.

▶

"It's good food not fine words that keep me alive"
Molière

CHOCOLATE

1 tablespoon Dietade Fruit Sugar
2 dessertspoons cocoa powder

4 tablespoons water
8 oz creamed coconut

Mix the fructose and cocoa together in a pan. Slowly add the water, stirring all the time. Put on a low heat and slowly bring to the boil. Chop up half the coconut block and add to the cocoa mixture. Stir over a low heat, adding more of the coconut until it becomes fairly thick. Also add more fructose if necessary, to taste. This can be spooned into little paper cases or those lovely little chocolate moulds. Leave to set in fridge.

Variation

Fruit and Nut Chocolates Into the thick coconut mixture, fold in 3 oz dried fruit and chopped nuts of choice. As the mixture starts to set, roll into balls and then roll in cocoa powder.

◄

CHOCOLATE ORANGE SWEETS

Candied Peel (see page 86)

Chocolate Topping (see page 85)

Take strips of peel and dip them halfway into the chocolate mixture so that they are half coated.

►

MARZIPAN DATES

2 quantities of Marzipan (see pages 85 and 86)

1 box dates with stones or 1 lb fresh dates

Split the dates and remove the stones. Fill with the marzipan.

BASIC SCONES

3 oz Granose margarine
8 oz plain flour
2 heaped teaspoons baking powder

¼ teaspoon cream of tartar
a little salt
water to mix

Rub the margarine into the flour, then add the baking powder, cream of tartar and salt. Handling as little as possible, mix with water to a soft dough – slightly softer than pastry. Turn on to a floured surface and roll out to about ¾ inch thick. Cut out with a cutter into rounds and put on to a baking sheet. Bake in a very hot oven, 230°C/450°F/Gas 8, for 10 minutes, no more. Eat at once, split and spread with Granose margarine and sugar-free jam or a savoury filling, if preferred.

Variations

Fruit Scones Add 3 oz dried fruit to the basic mixture.

Cinnamon Scones Add 1 teaspoon cinnamon to the basic mixture.

▶

DROP SCONES

6 oz plain flour
2 large eggs
water to mix
1 dessertspoon Dietade Fruit Sugar

a pinch of salt
1 tablespoon sunflower oil
1 drop pure vanilla essence

Put the flour into a basin, add the eggs and a little water (sufficient to be able to give the mixture a really good beating to knock the bumps out). Beat well, then add the other ingredients. Finally add enough water to make a very thick batter.

Lightly grease a large frying pan. Pour a tablespoon of mixture on to the hot pan and cook for a few minutes each side on a medium heat. Lift a corner to see if the drop scone is turning brown and if so, flip it over. You can probably cook three or four at a time depending on the size of your pan.

Serve hot with maple syrup poured over or serve cold and spread with Granose margarine and sugar-free jam.

FLAPJACKS

3 oz Granose margarine
2–3 tablespoons maple syrup
3 oz Dietade Fruit Sugar
2 large eggs

8 oz porridge oats
2 oz plain flour
3 oz dried fruit (of choice to include 1
    oz chopped dates)

Mix the margarine, syrup, fructose and eggs together well. Stir in the oats, flour and fruit. Put into a greased oblong tin. Bake in a moderate oven, 180°C/350°F/Gas 4, for 30 minutes. Leave to cool for 20 minutes and cut into fingers. Leave in the tin until cold before removing.

◀

APRICOT AND ALMOND TRUFFLES

4 oz ground almonds
4 oz cake crumbs from a Basic Sponge
    (see page 81)
2 tablespoons Apricot Jam (see page
    106)

3 oz Dietade Fruit Sugar
a little Maison l'Heraud brandy
1 quantity Chocolate Topping (see
    page 85)
split almonds to decorate

Mix all the ingredients (except the chocolate topping) together with the brandy to make a really thick paste. Make into cherry-sized balls, put on to a polythene sheet and put into the freezer for about 1 hour.
    Make the chocolate topping.
    Remove the almond mixture from the freezer. Put a small amount of chocolate topping into tiny paper cases, the balls of almond mixture on to the chocolate and then cover them all with more chocolate topping. Put a split almond on to each one to decorate. Keep in the fridge.

▶

Man did eat Angel's food
(Psalms)

MARZIPAN FRUITS

1 quantity Marzipan (see pages 85 and 86)
fresh fruit pureé or sugar-free jam

food colouring

Mix the marzipan with fresh fruit pureé or jam and mould into fruit shapes. Use colouring as well for artistic effect.

For pears cut a clove in half and put the star piece at the bottom and the stick at the top for the stalk.

For apples paint the food colouring on one side to give an authentic look.

Paint brown lines down the sides of the bananas.

Roll strawberry shapes over the smallest sized grater (the nutmeg grater) to give the strawberry effect.

◀

UPSIDE-DOWN CAKE

285g can sugar-free fruit of choice
1 dessertspoon Dietade Fruit Sugar

1 quantity Basic Sponge Mixture (see page 81)
2 oz Granose margarine

Drain the fruit and reserve the juice. Melt the margarine in a pan, add the fructose, stir until dissolved. Pour into a greased, solid-bottomed, 8 inch tin or dish. Arrange the fruit in the melted margarine. Pour over the sponge mixture, in a moderate oven, 180°C/350°F/Gas 4, for 35 minutes.

While the cake is baking, reduce the fruit syrup to about 3 tablespoons by boiling rapidly. Leave the cake to cool slightly in the tin for about 15 minutes. Before removing, spear the sponge with a skewer in several places and then gently pour over the reduced syrup. Remove the cake from the tin while it is still warm.

COFFEE AND HAZELNUT GÂTEAU

1 quantity coffee-flavoured Fatless Sponge (see **Note** and page 81)

2 quantities Coffee Cream Filling (see page 84)
4 oz hazelnuts, finely chopped

Make the sponge, adding the coffee at the end. Spread into a greased and lined 11 x 16 inch Swiss roll tin. Bake in a hot oven, 220°C/425°F/Gas 7, for about 10 minutes. Allow to cool.

Cut the sponge across into four 4 inch wide slices. Sandwich the slices together with the coffee cream filling, leaving enough filling to spread over the sides and to pipe on the top as decoration. Scatter the hazelnuts over the top and sides.

Note To flavour the sponge, dissolve 1 tablespoon instant coffee in 1 dessertspoon boiling water and leave to cool, then fold this into the basic sponge mixture at the end.

◀

COFFEE HAZELNUT TART

1 quantity Almond Pastry (see page 83)
3 large eggs
4 oz Dietade Fruit Sugar
3 oz Granose margarine

¼ pint water mixed with 3 teaspoons instant coffee (decaffeinated)
2 teaspoons gelatine
3 oz tofu (bean curd), blended if necessary
2 oz chopped hazelnuts

Line an 8 inch pie plate with the pastry, prick the base and bake blind in a fairly hot oven, 200°C/400°F/Gas 6, for 15 minutes.

Put the eggs, fructose and margarine and half the coffee mixture in a heatproof bowl over a pan of boiling water or in the top of a double boiler. Stir until the mixture starts to thicken. Dissolve the gelatine in the remaining coffee mixture and add to the egg mixture. Stir in the blended tofu and the nuts.

Pour into the pastry case. Leave to set.

White Bread Dough (page 101) made into various shapes.

CHAPTER EIGHT

BREAD

▲

WHITE BREAD

MAKES THREE 1 LB LOAVES

4 oz Granose margarine
3 lb strong white bread flour (see **Note**)
3 teaspoons salt

2 oz fresh yeast
1 teaspoon Dietade Fruit Sugar
about 1½ pints warm water to mix

Rub the margarine into the flour, then add the salt. Put the fresh yeast into a measuring jug and add the fructose, then crumble the yeast with a fork to mix the two together. Leave to stand for about 10 minutes by which time the yeast will have become runny. Add ½ pint warmish water to the yeast and stir very well. Tip this on to the flour, then add ½ pint very warm water and start to mix it in, adding more warm water if necessary to make a soft dough.

Knead for 10 minutes by hand, or for 5 minutes if using a mixer with a dough hook. Cover the bowl with an oiled polythene bag and leave to stand in a warm place. A good idea is to stand the bowl in a larger bowl with a couple of pints of boiling water in the larger bowl surrounding the dough bowl. If the yeast is very fresh the dough should be well risen in 30 minutes. Wait until it has doubled in size.

Turn on to a floured surface and weigh the dough. This quantity of dough will make three loaves, so divide it into three. If you are going to put it into loaf tins, flatten each piece of dough to an oblong shape, with your hands and then tightly roll it up, swiss roll fashion, tucking the ends in. This way it rises better. Put into loaf tins.

If you want to make a round loaf, then you must knead and tighten the dough into a nice ball shape, otherwise it will spread out too much. Cover the dough with oiled polythene and leave for about 30 minutes to rise again, until just double in size. Some people think that the longer the dough is left the better, but if the dough is allowed to over-rise it will fall down into itself in the oven and end up flat.

Bake (see **Note**) in a very hot oven, 230°C/450°F/Gas 8, for about 25 minutes, until golden brown.

continued

Note Go to your baker and beg him to sell you some strong white bread flour, preferably Canadian.

Note Always preheat the oven when cooking or baking. This is very important, particularly in bread making, so make sure the oven is very hot before the bread goes in!

Note From this basic dough you can make various shaped loaves such as a Cottage loaf and a Plaited loaf.

Variations

Rye Bread Follow the basic white bread recipe but substitute 2 lb strong white bread flour and 1 lb rye flour for the 3 lb flour.

Continental Rye Proceed as in the basic recipe, but substitute 2 lb 12 oz strong white bread flour and 4 oz rye flour for the 3 lb flour. Brush the surface of the dough with a little oil before baking.

Wholemeal Bread Proceed as in the basic recipe but substitute 2 lb wholemeal flour and 1 lb strong white bread flour for the 3 lb flour.

Onion Herb Bread Follow the basic recipe, but substitute 2 lb 12 oz strong white bread flour and 4 oz rye flour for the 3 lb flour (as when making Continental Rye). Add to the flour: 1 very finely chopped onion, 1 crushed garlic clove, 1 teaspoon chopped fresh parsley and ½ teaspoon dried rosemary. Brush the dough with a little oil before baking.

Fruit Bread Put 6 oz mixed dried fruit into a basin, cover with very hot water and leave to stand for 30 minutes. Drain. Make up ½ quantity basic White Bread dough; but before adding the yeast and water to the flour, mix in the fruit with 2 dessertspoons Dietade Fruit Sugar and a little mixed spice. Proceed as for basic recipe.

▲

BREAD ROLLS

MAKES ABOUT 16

½ quantity basic bread dough of your choice

poppy seeds, caraway seeds and sesame seeds to decorate (optional)

Prepare the dough and then weigh it out into 2 oz balls. Knead each ball into a tight little round and place the balls an inch apart on a greased baking tray. If liked you can decorate the tops of the rolls with a sprinkling of seeds. Bake in a very hot oven, 230°C/450°F/Gas 8, for about 10–15 minutes.

STOLLEN

double quantity of Marzipan (see pages 85 and 86)
4 oz mixed Candied Peel (see page 86)
5 oz sultanas
3 oz currants
2 tablespoons Maison l'Heraud brandy or fresh orange juice
1 lb strong white bread flour
¾ oz fresh yeast

7 oz Dietade Fruit Sugar plus a little for sprinkling
10 fl oz water
1 large egg
grated zest of 1 lemon
3½ oz melted Granose margarine, plus ½ oz softened
1 oz blanched almonds, crushed or slivered
a few drops of almond essence

Make the marzipan and put in a cool place. Make the candied peel. Soak the sultanas and currants in the brandy or orange juice overnight.

The next day, sift half the flour into a bowl and put the yeast into a measuring jug. Add a little of the fructose and crumble the yeast with a fork to mix. Add 6 fl oz of the water to the yeast and mix thoroughly. Leave until the yeast is dissolved, then add to the flour and mix thoroughly. Cover with a damp cloth and leave to rise in a warm place, until it has doubled in size.

Put the peel into a blender with 4 fl oz of the water and blend until the peel is well chopped up – we do this because we don't like big pieces of peel; if preferred, just chop the peel with a knife and add to the water.

Beat the egg, lemon zest and remaining fructose together and add 3 oz melted margarine. Add the egg mixture to the risen dough with the remaining flour, the candied peel and the water.

Knead the dough until it comes together, then knead for a further 10 minutes by hand or for 5 minutes if using a mixer with a dough hook. Dot with the softened margarine, cover with a clean damp cloth and leave to rise in a warm place until doubled in size.

Knead the dough briefly. Drain the fruit and reserve the brandy or orange juice. Add the fruit to the dough and knead it in.

Roll the dough out to a large oval shape. Roll the marzipan out to fit the length and half the width of the dough shape, then set aside. Brush the surface of the dough with the reserved brandy or orange juice. Sprinkle the crushed or slivered almonds over the surface. Place the marzipan on one half of the dough oval and fold the dough over to meet the opposite edge, pinching the edges together well to form a huge turnover. Brush with some melted margarine and place on a well greased baking sheet. Leave to rise until doubled in size.

Bake on the centre shelf in a fairly hot oven, 200°C/400°F/Gas 6, for about 15 minutes. After 15 minutes, cover with foil to prevent the Stollen becoming too brown. Bake for a further 15 minutes or until a skewer comes out clean. When the Stollen comes out of the oven, generously brush the top with a little melted margarine mixed with almond essence. Sprinkle over a little fructose, to finish.

A selection of fruit jellies.

CHAPTER NINE

PRESERVES

◄

We have found that jam making is as good with fruit sugar, as with ordinary sugar. The jams will keep well for a few weeks but it is best to refrigerate after opening.

If you want to convert your own recipes to use fructose, simply halve the amount of fructose for sugar. Thus, for example, use 4 oz Dietade Fruit Sugar instead of 8 oz sugar.

To aid storage, add 2 crushed Campden Tablets to each pound of fruit – the tablets inhibit fermentation in these sugar-free jams by killing off yeasts. Campden Tablets are available from home-made wine making departments.

Always make sure that you cook the fruit well at the start of the jam making to release the pectin fully, before adding the fructose; once you have added the fructose it inhibits the pectin release from the fruit. This stage of cooking may take about an hour but depends on the type of fruit.

Ann has a good test for pectin: if you drop a little of the cooked fruit into some methylated spirits and it jellifies, there is sufficient pectin in the liquid for you to add the fructose and continue with the recipe.

If you have a pressure cooker, this is an ideal way to cook the fruit – but halve the fluid.

After adding the fructose the jam will usually need cooking for another 15 minutes or so to reach setting point but again this will vary from recipe to recipe.

To test for setting: use a teaspoon and drop a small amount of the jam on to a cold plate, push the jam with your fingertip and if it wrinkles it is ready.

After potting in clean warm jars, we use waxed discs on the hot jams and then transparent covers. An alternative method of sealing is to pour melted paraffin wax on top of the cold jams in the jars.

▼

"Kissing don't last: Cookery do!"
George Meredith

APRICOT JAM

1 lb dried apricots, chopped and
  soaked overnight in 2½ pints water
1 lb Dietade Fruit Sugar
grated rind and juice of 2 lemons
2 oz almonds, blanched and chopped

1 tablespoon Maison l'Heraud brandy
  (optional)
2 Campden Tablets, crushed
½ oz Granose margarine

Put the soaked apricots and water into a pan, bring to the boil and simmer gently for 30 minutes or until the fruit is soft.

Add the fructose and stir until it is dissolved. Bring back to the boil and boil rapidly for 15–20 minutes, then add the lemon rind and juice.

Continue to cook until a soft setting point is reached. Remove from heat, add the almonds and brandy and then add the Campden Tablets and margarine. Stir well until Campden Tablets are dissolved. Pot into jars and cover.

▼

MEDLAR JAM

3 lb medlars, skinned and cores
  removed (see **Note**)
½ pint water

Dietade Fruit Sugar
vanilla pod or pure vanilla essence
6 Campden Tablets, crushed

Put the medlars into a pan with the water and mash well with a potato masher or fork. Bring to the boil and simmer for about 30 minutes until soft.

Allow to cool slightly and put through a sieve. Weigh the pulp and for every pound of pulp add 6 oz Dietade Fruit Sugar. Stir well until the fructose has dissolved, then add the vanilla pod or essence. Boil until the setting point is reached. Remove the vanilla pod if using. Remove the jam from the heat and add the Campden Tablets, stirring until dissolved. Pot and cover.

Note Fruit for this jam should be over-ripe.

◄

"Heaven sends us good meat, but the Devil sends cooks".
David Garrick

MULBERRY JAM

2 lb mulberries
¼ pint water
2 tablespoons lemon juice

1 lb Dietade Fruit Sugar
4 Campden Tablets, crushed

Remove the stalks and any blemishes from the fruit. Put the fruit into a pan with the water. Cook gently over a low heat until the juice runs.

Add the lemon juice and simmer for about 15 minutes.

Add the fructose and stir well, boil until the setting point is reached. Remove from the heat and add the Campden Tablets, stirring until dissolved. Pot and cover.

▶

MIRABELLE AND DATE PRESERVE

1 lb mirabelles (or plums or damsons)
water
12 oz Date Syrup (see page 23)

3 tablespoons Dietade Fruit Sugar
a little cornflour (optional)

Gently cook the mirabelles in water to cover. Allow to cool and remove the stones. Add the date syrup and fructose. Cook gently together. If the jam is too runny, add a little cornflour mixed in a little cold water. Pot and cover; keep refrigerated.

◀

PLUM AND WALNUT CHEESE

2¼ lb plums
½ pint water
1 lb Dietade Fruit Sugar

4 Campden Tablets, crushed
4 oz walnuts, chopped

Cook the plums in the water for about 30 minutes. Allow to cool.

Remove the stones and blend the fruit in a blender until smooth.

Add the fructose and bring to the boil until setting point is reached. Remove from the heat, add the Campden Tablets and walnuts, pot and cover.

SLOE AND APPLE CHEESE

1 lb cooking apples, such as Bramley's
1 lb ripe sloes (these are best after the
    first frost)

water to cover
Dietade Fruit Sugar
4 Campden Tablets, crushed

Core the apples, leaving the peel on; put the cores including pips in a muslin bag. Put the apples, sloes and muslin bag into a pan. Barely cover with water, bring to the boil and simmer for about 30 minutes. Allow to cool.

Remove the stones and the muslin bag, squeezing the juice from it. Put the fruit and all the juice into blender and blend until smooth. Weigh the pulp and add 7 oz Dietade Fruit Sugar for every pound of fruit.

Bring back to the boil and boil until setting point is reached. Remove from the heat and add the Campden Tablets, stirring until dissolved. Pot and cover.

▶

DAMSON CHEESE

4 lb damsons
1 pint water

2 lb Dietade Fruit Sugar
8 Campden Tablets, crushed

Cook the fruit in the water for about 30 minutes or until soft. Allow to cool.

Remove the stones. Put the fruit and juice into a blender and blend until smooth.

Return to the pan, add the fructose and boil until setting point is reached. Remove from the heat and add the Campden Tablets, stirring until dissolved. Pot and cover.

◀

When our editor came to see us she said that "some cooks make the food look like a cat's breakfast". When Ann got home and repeated it to her family, they chorused "and did she live?"

APPLE JELLY

6 lb cooking apples, such as Bramley's
water to cover

thinly pared rind of 2 lemons
Dietade Fruit Sugar
12 Campden Tablets, crushed

Cut apples into thick rings and cover with water. Add the thinly pared rind of the lemons. Boil until the fruit is pulpy. Cool slightly.

Pour into a jelly bag and leave overnight for the juice to drip into a container.

Measure the juice and add 7 oz Dietade Fruit Sugar for every pint. Bring to the boil and boil until setting point is reached. Remove from the heat, add the Campden Tablets and stir until dissolved. Pot and cover.

Variations

Herb Jellies   Divide the juice between several pans; add a sprig of sage to one, a sprig of thyme to another and a sprig of rosemary to another and so on. This makes lovely deep red jellies. Add sprigs of herbs to the pots too, before covering.

◀

QUINCE JELLY

quinces
Dietade Fruit Sugar

water to cover
Campden Tablets, crushed

Pare and slice the quinces and put into pan, barely cover with water and boil until the fruit is soft.

Cool for 1 hour. Pour into a jelly bag and suspend over a bowl (I tie mine to the four legs of an upside-down stool. Leave overnight or until all the juice has dripped through.

Measure the juice and for each pint add 7 oz Dietade Fruit Sugar.

Boil until setting point is reached. Remove from the heat and add 2 Campden Tablets for each pint of juice. Stir well until dissolved. Pot and cover.

LEMON CURD

2 large eggs
rind and juice of 1 lemon

2 oz Granose margarine
2 oz Dietade Fruit Sugar

Put all the ingredients into the top of a double saucepan, or in a heatproof bowl in a pan of simmering water. Stir continuously and heat until the sugar has dissolved and the curd thickens – do make sure that it is really thick.

Alternatively, put all of the ingredients into a heatproof bowl and mix well. Cover with a piece of greaseproof paper and cook at 15 lb (High) pressure for 10 minutes in a pressure cooker with water around the bowl. Take from the pressure cooker and beat vigourously with a balloon whisk: the curd will thicken as it cools.

To store the lemon curd, pour into small sterilised jars and cover as for jam. The lemon curd will only keep for about a month.

▶

PICKLED WALNUTS

young green walnuts
water
salt
spiced vinegar
malt vinegar

peppercorns
allspice berries
fresh root ginger
cloves

Prick the walnuts all over with a carpet needle or other large needle, wear rubber gloves for this or the walnuts will stain your hands black and the stain will not wash out for days!

Put the walnuts into a bowl and cover with brine (dissolve 6 oz salt in each ¼ pint water needed to cover). Leave for 6 days, strain and cover with fresh brine and leave for another 6 days.

Drain the walnuts and lie them on a rack to dry in the sun if possible – this recipe works well in the South of France!

Alternatively, you can leave the nuts to dry in a warm airing cupboard. When the walnuts are fully dry, they should be black.

To make the spiced vinegar, to each 2 pints malt vinegar you are using, you will need 1 oz peppercorns, 2 oz allspice, 1 oz fresh root ginger and 12 cloves. Simmer the spices in 1 pint of the vinegar for 10 minutes, then strain into the remaining 1 pint vinegar.

Put the dried blackened walnuts in jars and pour over the spiced vinegar to cover. Seal the jars. The pickled walnuts will be ready to eat in 2–3 months.

RUNNER BEAN CURRIED PICKLE

2 lb runner beans, sliced
1 lb onions, chopped
½ pint water
1 pint malt vinegar
1 tablespoon salt

5 oz Dietade Fruit Sugar
1 tablespoon curry powder
2 tablespoons cornflour or more to thicken

Put the beans and onions in a pan with the water and cook for 10 minutes, then drain.

Put the vegetables back into the pan and add all but 2 tablespoons of the vinegar. Add the salt and fructose and bring to the boil. Boil for 5 minutes; then remove the pan from the heat and allow to cool for a moment or two.

Mix the curry powder with the cornflour and the 2 tablespoons vinegar. Whip the cornflour mixture into the pan.

Bring back to the boil and boil for about 4 minutes, stirring all the time. If the mixture is not thick enough, add more cornflour. Allow to cool slightly, pot and cover.

▶

PICCALILLI – I

2 lb runner beans, sliced
4 or 5 onions, chopped
1½ pints malt vinegar
2 tablespoons cornflour
1 oz mustard powder

3 teaspoons turmeric
¼ pint water
2 teaspoons salt
about 5 oz Dietade Fruit Sugar

Put the beans in a pan of water with the onions. Boil for 10 minutes, then drain.

Return the onions and beans to the pan, add the vinegar and bring to the boil.

Mix the cornflour, mustard powder and turmeric together and mix with the water and salt. Stir well. Remove the pan from the heat and stir in the cornflour mixture. Add fructose to taste.

Bring back to the boil and simmer for 10 minutes, stirring all the time. Allow to cool slightly. Pot and cover.

Variation

Piccalilli – II Follow the basic recipe but instead of the green beans, use a mixture of green beans, cauliflower florets and sliced baby cucumber.

CORN RELISH

1 lb white cabbage, shredded
2 onions, chopped
8 oz red and green peppers, chopped
1 lb sweetcorn kernels
2 pints spiced vinegar

4 oz Dietade Fruit Sugar
2 teaspoons salt
1 tablespoon mustard powder
2 heaped tablespoons cornflour
4 tablespoons water

Put all the ingredients except the mustard, cornflour and water into a pan.
Bring to the boil and simmer for 20 minutes. Remove from heat.

Mix the mustard and cornflour together with the water. Add to the pan and return to the heat. Bring back to the boil and simmer for 10 minutes, stirring all the time. Pot and cover.

▲

GREEN TOMATO CHUTNEY

2 lb green tomatoes, chopped
2 large onions, chopped
2 large apples, chopped
1 tablespoon salt
2 tablespoons mixed pickling spice
    (tied in a muslin bag)

4 oz Dietade Fruit Sugar
½ inch fresh root ginger, chopped
4 garlic cloves, crushed
2 teaspoons chopped fresh green
    chillies
1½ pints malt vinegar

Put all the ingredients into a pan and simmer until everything is soft.
Remove the muslin bag. Pot and cover, or freeze.

◄

HARVEST CHUTNEY

4 lb cooking apples, such as
    Bramley's, peeled, cored and
    chopped
1 lb pears
2 lb tomatoes
1 lb plums, stoned
2 lb onions, chopped

½ oz garlic, chopped
1 dessertspoon chopped green chilli
2 pints malt vinegar
2 tablespoons mixed pickling spice
    (tied in a muslin bag)
1 oz salt
8 oz Dietade Fruit Sugar

Put all the ingredients into a pan and simmer until very thick. Remove the muslin bag. Pot and cover, or freeze.

MARROW CHUTNEY

3 lb marrow or courgettes, skinned
   and deseeded
salt
1 lb onions, finely chopped
1 lb cooking apples, such as
   Bramley's, peeled and cored
1 oz mixed spice tied in muslin bag

½ inch fresh root ginger, chopped
1 level teaspoon chilli powder
4 oz sultanas
3 oz Dietade Fruit Sugar
2 pints malt vinegar
6 oz chopped nuts (optional)

Cube the marrow, spread on a flat dish and sprinkle with salt. Allow to stand overnight to draw out the water. Rinse the marrow well and put into a large pan. Add all the other ingredients and bring to the boil. Simmer for about 30 minutes until fairly thick. Remove the muslin bag. Pot and cover, or freeze.

Note This is a delicious solution to an embarrassment of marrows or courgettes.

◀

TAMARIND CHUTNEY

1 lb onions, chopped
2 garlic cloves, chopped
½ inch fresh root ginger, chopped
about 2 tablespoons tamarind purée
   (see **Note**)

2 tablespoons malt vinegar
about 2 tablespoons Dietade Fruit
   Sugar
water to cover

Put all the ingredients into a pan and cook until mushy and squashy.
   Taste the chutney to see if it needs more fructose or more tamarind purée.
   If you like a very smooth chutney, then pop it in the blender and blend until smooth. Pot and cover, or freeze.

Note Tamarind purée is obtainable from Health Food shops.

▶

"He watches his diet carefully, he looks at every forkful as it goes in his mouth." (Ann about Alvin, Liza's husband)

SPICED ORANGE AND PEAR CHUTNEY

4 lb pears, peeled, cored and chopped
2 lb onions, chopped
1 inch fresh root ginger, chopped
juice and rind of 2 oranges
1 tablespoon mixed spice (in a muslin
  bag)

1 tablespoon salt
5 oz Dietade Fruit Sugar
1 garlic clove, crushed
1 pint malt vinegar

Put all the ingredients into a pan and cook until soft and mushy. Remove the muslin bag. Pot and cover, or freeze.

◄

MARMALADE

1 lb oranges, Seville if possible
2 pints water
1 lemon

1 lb Dietade Fruit Sugar
3 Campden Tablets, crushed

Wash the fruit, cut in half and squeeze the juice, retaining the juice and pips. Cut the thick membrane and some of the white pith coating from inside the peel; tie up this membrane and pith in a muslin bag with the pips. If you want you can at this point freeze everything until you are ready to make the marmalade, it makes the peel softer too.

Cut up the peel and put with the juice, a pint of the water and the muslin bag in a bowl. Stand overnight.

The next day put the contents of the bowl with the remaining pint of water into a large pan. Simmer for 45 minutes until the peel is tender.

Remove from the heat and add the fructose. Stir until dissolved and return to the heat.

Boil rapidly until setting point is reached. Remove from the heat, stir in the Camden Tablets until dissolved. Remove the muslin bag. Pot and cover.

◄

"She's on a seafood diet – sees food and eats it."
(Alvin about Ann)

MIXED FRUIT MARMALADE

1 grapefruit
2 oranges
8 kumquats
2 limes

2 lemons
water
Dietade Fruit Sugar
3 Campden Tablets, crushed

Wash the fruit. Cut the kumquats horizontally into small rounds and cut all the other fruit vertically into fine segments, saving all the pips and juice. Tie the pips up in a muslin bag. Put all the fruit and juice into a bowl, barely cover with water and leave overnight.

The next day put the contents of the bowl into a pan with the muslin bag. Boil until the skins are tender. Allow to cool and remove the muslin bag.

Measure the fruit and to every pint of fruit stir in 8 oz Dietade Fruit Sugar.

Return to the heat and boil until it reaches setting point. Remove from the heat and stir in the Campden Tablets until dissolved. Pot and cover. This is a yummy chunky marmalade.

▶

MINCEMEAT

1 teaspoon grated nutmeg
3 teaspoons mixed spice
1 teaspoon ground cloves (optional)
1 teaspoon cinnamon
1½ lb beef suet, shredded
4 oz Date Syrup (see page 23)
4 fl oz Maison l'Heraud brandy
   (optional)
1 lb raisins
1 lb sultanas
1 lb currants

8 oz mixed candied peel (see page 86),
   finely chopped
4 oz dried peaches, chopped
4 oz dried pears, chopped
4 oz dried figs, chopped
4 oz almonds, chopped
1 lb chopped apple
grated rind and juice of 2 lemons
4 oz Dietade Fruit Sugar
3 tablespoons sugar-free apple juice
   concentrate

Mix the fructose and spices together, add the suet and mix well. Add the date syrup and the brandy if using. Add all the other ingredients and mix very well. It is good to give every member of the family a stir and they can each make a wish, too. Cover and leave to stand for 2 days, stirring when the mood takes you.

Pot into clean, dry jars, place a waxed disc on top and seal. This mincemeat is ready for immediate use; keep refrigerated. For storing, freeze in containers.

Sophie's Birthday Party.

CHAPTER TEN

SOPHIE'S BIRTHDAY PARTY

◄

VEGETABLE STICKS

Chop any fresh vegetables into sticks: use cucumber, celery, carrot, courgettes, red and green peppers, spring onions, runner beans, mangetout, asparagus, in fact anything you like. Make a selection of dips and serve with raw vegetables.

◄

MAYONNAISE DIP

2 large eggs
salt and pepper
1 teaspoon mustard powder
6 fl oz sunflower oil

6 fl oz olive oil
lemon juice and white wine vinegar
flavouring of choice

Mix the egg yolks, salt and pepper and mustard together very well until light and creamy, gradually add the oil, drop by drop. When all the oil is added, add some lemon juice and/or white wine vinegar. If the mayonnaise is too thick, add a little boiling water. You can flavour the dip with a little tomato purée and crushed garlic or chopped gherkins, capers and a little parsley.

CURRIED MAYONNAISE DIP

Make ½ quantity Curried Mayonnaise (see page 17)

▲

AVOCADO DIP

1 avocado, peeled and stoned
½ quantity (½ pint) Mayonnaise (see
    page 17)

a little extra lemon juice

Mix all the ingredients in a blender until well combined. Make this dip just before serving as the avocado can discolour.

▶

TARAMASALATA AND AVOCADO DIP

2 slices of white bread, crusts
    removed
about 3 fl oz olive oil
about 3 fl oz sunflower oil
1 garlic clove

3 oz smoked cod's roe, cut into pieces
    with membranes and skin removed
juice of ½ lemon
salt and pepper
1 avocado

Soak the bread in water. Put half the oil into a liquidiser goblet and add the garlic clove and the roe. Squeeze the water from the bread, but leave moist. Add to the goblet. Start the machine running and dribble the remaining oil in slowly until the mixture is of a smooth very thick consistency. Add the lemon juice, salt and pepper to make taramasalata.

Peel and stone the avocado and mash with a fork, Add this to the taramasalata.

Note The taramasalata without the avocado added, makes a good starter served with toast.

SAUSAGES ON STICKS

1½ lb minced pork
1 onion, minced
4 oz fresh fine white breadcrumbs
1 teaspoon each chopped fresh sage,
    thyme, marjoram and parsley

1½ teaspooons salt
½ teaspoon pepper
a little stock

Mix all the ingredients together, adding a little stock to make the mixture soft enough to go through a sausage-making machine. If you have no sausage-making machine, mould into sausage shapes with floured hands. Fry or grill until cooked. Serve hot or cold on cocktail sticks.

◄

EGG AND BACON CROQUETTES

3 oz chopped onion
2 oz Granose margarine
2 tablespoons plain flour
½ pint sugar-free chicken stock
3 large hard-boiled eggs, finely
    chopped
4 bacon rashers, crisply fried and
    chopped

1 large egg (raw)
1 tablespoon water
salt and pepper
fine breadcrumbs to coat
sunflower oil for deep frying

Sweat the onion in the margarine in a pan. Remove the onion and reserve. Add the flour to the melted margarine and stir well. Remove the pan from the heat and slowly add the chicken stock. Return to the heat and stir for 2 minutes. Bring to the boil, stirring all the time. Add the hard-boiled eggs, bacon and reserved onion to the sauce. Pour on to a plate and leave to cool. The sauce should be very thick.

When the sauce mixture is quite cold, place on a floured surface and roll dessertspoons of the mixture into balls. Beat the raw egg with 1 tablespoon water and salt and pepper. Roll the balls in the egg mixture and then in the breadcrumbs.

Deep fry in very hot sunflower oil until golden. Drain on kitchen paper.

SANDWICHES

Read the labels and buy bread made without sugar and whey, or make your own.

Spread the bread slices with Granose margarine.

Spread with Marmite, sugar-free jam, sugar-free peanut butter, slices of cucumber or hard-boiled eggs mixed with a little home-made Mayonnaise (see page 17).

◀

CUP CAKES

2 large eggs
4 oz creamed coconut, grated
4 oz Granose margarine

about 4 tablespoons sugar-free apple
   juice
4 oz sponge flour
selected toppings of your choice

Put the eggs into a liquidiser goblet, add the grated coconut cream and run the liquidiser for 30 seconds. Add the margarine and blend for another 30 seconds. Add 2 tablespoons of the apple juice.

Sieve the flour into a bowl, fold in the creamy mixture and add just enough apple juice to give a dropping consistency.

Put dessertspoonfuls of the mixture into individual paper cases – this amount is about right as the cakes do not rise very much.

Bake in a moderate oven, 180°C/350°F/Gas 4, for about 15 minutes. The cup cakes will still be pale in colour as they do not go brown when cooked.

Cover the cup cakes with your favourite toppings. We like to use the following: a little sugar-free jam and long strand coconut; a spoonful of Lemon Curd (see page 110); or a little Chocolate Topping (see page 85).

Variations

Chocolate Cup Cakes Add 1 dessertspoon cocoa powder to the basic mixture.

Almond Cup Cakes Add ½ teaspoon almond essence to the basic mixture.

Fruit Cup Cakes Add 2 oz currants to the basic mixture.

Coconut Cup Cakes Add 1 dessertspoon desiccated coconut to the basic mixture.

CHELSEA BUNS

MAKES ABOUT 16

¾ oz fresh yeast
a pinch of Dietade Fruit Sugar
½ pint warm water
1 lb strong plain bread flour
1 oz sugar-free cooking fat such as
    Trex

Spiced Fruit Filling:
2 tablespoons Date Syrup (see page
    23) plus extra to glaze
1 teaspoon each mixed spice and
    grated nutmeg
4 oz mixed raisins, sultanas or
    currants

Put the yeast into a measuring jug and sprinkle over the fructose. Mix with a fork, then leave to stand for 10 minutes. Add the warm water, stir very well and leave to stand until the yeast starts to foam a little. Sieve the flour into a large bowl and rub in the cooking fat. Add the foamed yeast mixture, adding a little more liquid if necessary to make a soft dough. Knead for 10 minutes, or use a mixer with a dough hook and mix for 5 minutes. Cover with oiled polythene or cling film and put in a warm place for about 1 hour until doubled in size.

When the dough has doubled in size, turn out on to a floured surface and roll out to a rectangle about ¼ inch thick. Now coat with the filling. Using a pastry brush, paint the surface with the 2 tablespoons Date Syrup. Sprinkle the spices and scatter the fruit evenly over the surface.

Roll up, Swiss roll fashion, from a long edge. Cut into rounds about 1½ inches thick and place side-by-side in a greased roasting tin, or in any tin with sides. Leave to rise for about 30 minutes.

Bake in a very hot oven, 240°C/425°F/Gas 9, for about 12–15 minutes. Mix a little Date Syrup with boiling water and brush over the warm buns to glaze.

▲

FANCY BISCUITS

1 quantity Rich Pastry (see page 84)
a few currants

1 quantity Chocolate Topping (see
    page 85) optional

Make the pastry and roll out on to a floured surface, then cut with animal-shaped cutters and add currants for eyes. Place on a greased baking tray and bake in a fairly hot oven, 200°C/400°F/Gas 6, for 6 minutes. You can dip the biscuits in chocolate topping to add variety if liked. This pastry breaks very easily so be sure to handle the biscuits with care.

DOUGHNUT MICE

MAKES ABOUT 10

½ oz fresh yeast
a pinch of Dietade Fruit Sugar
4 tablespoons very warm water
1 large egg, beaten
2 oz sugar-free cooking fat such as
    Trex

8 oz strong plain bread flour
sunflower oil for deep frying
split almonds and currants to decorate

Cream the yeast and fructose with a fork. Add the warm water and beaten egg. Rub the cooking fat into the flour and add the yeast mixture. Knead for 10 minutes by hand or for 5 minutes if using a mixer with a dough hook. Leave with an oiled polythene bag over the top in a warm place until doubled in size.

Turn the risen dough out on to a floured surface. Form the dough into a longish roll and cut off pieces each weighing about an ounce. Make each piece into a ball, then pinch one side between thumb and finger to make a nose effect. Leave on a floured board in a warm place for about 30 minutes to rise.

Deep fry the doughnuts in hot sunflower oil for 8 minutes, turning once. The doughnuts will remain pale in colour when cooked as they do not go as brown as ordinary doughnuts. Drain and leave to cool completely.

When cold, make a slit in the bottom of each doughnut and fill with sugar-free jam.

Make into mice with split almonds for ears, currants for eyes and nose and a little piece of string with a knot in it for the tail.

Variations

Cream Doughnuts Simply roll the dough pieces into balls instead of shaping into mice. These are delightful, filled with sugar-free jam and Cream Filling (see page 84).

Chocolate Cream Doughnuts Make the cream doughnuts and then coat with Chocolate Topping (see page 85) to finish.

◄

"Who doth ambition shun
And loves to live i the sun
Seeking the food he eats
And pleased with what he gets"
Shakespeare 'As You Like It'

LEMON CURD TARTS

1 quantity Rich Pastry(see page 84) Lemon Curd (see page 110) to fill the tarts

Roll out the pastry on a floured surface, cut out rounds and use to line tartlet tins. Prick the bases with a fork. Bake blind in a fairly hot oven, 200°C/400°F/Gas 6, for about 6 minutes. Cool and fill with lemon curd.

Variations

Jam Tarts Fill the pastry cases with sugar-free jam. Bake for 10 minutes.

Bakewell Tarts Make the pastry cases and spoon a little sugar-free jam into the centre of each tart, then top with 1 teaspoon Cup Cake mixture (see page 120) flavoured with a little almond essence. Bake for about 10–15 minutes.

▼

APRICOT SPONGE CAKE

1 quantity Basic Sponge (see page 81)

FILLING:

4 oz dried apricots soaked overnight in 6 oz sugar-free apple juice plus extra if needed (see **Note**)
3 oz Granose margarine

2 tablespoons flour
½ pint soya milk
1 dessertspoon Dietade Fruit Sugar
2 teaspoons pure vanilla essence

Bake the sponge, turn out and leave to cool on a wire rack. Split in half when cold.

To make the filling, simmer the soaked apricots in the apple juice until very soft. Add more apple juice if necessary. Purée in a blender or rub through a sieve.

Melt the margarine in a pan and add the flour. Slowly add the milk, stirring all the time. Cook for 2 minutes, stirring all the time, to make a very thick sauce. Add the fructose and vanilla essence. Fold in the apricot mixture. Leave to cool.

Fill the cake with the cooled apricot filling. Serve with a little dried unsweetened soya milk sprinkled over the top of the cake to give the effect of icing sugar.

Note Be sure to soak the apricots thoroughly before making the filling.

CHOCOLATE MOUSSE

3 heaped teaspoons gelatine
3 tablespoons water
2 teaspoons instant coffee
½ pint soya milk
1 dessertspoon cocoa powder
4 large eggs, separated
½ pint sunflower oil

3 heaped dessertspoons Dietade Fruit
   Sugar
a few finely chopped hazelnuts
   (optional)
1 quantity Chocolate Topping (see
   page 85)

Put the gelatine into the 3 tablespoons water in a heatproof bowl and leave to stand for 5 minutes until spongy. Stand the bowl in a pan of simmering water until the gelatine is quite dissolved. Add the instant coffee to the gelatine.

Pour the milk into a saucepan, sprinkle over the cocoa powder and leave for 10 minutes. Slowly bring to the boil, remove from the heat and allow to cool slightly. Add the gelatine and coffee mixture. Put the chocolate mixture into the fridge and leave until it is just starting to set. Do not allow it to become too firm or the mousse will go lumpy. Meanwhile, very slowly cream the egg yolks and add the sunflower oil drop by drop to form a thick cream.

When the chocolate mixture is just starting to set, remove it from the fridge and stir in the fructose. Add the oil cream, stirring well to combine. Whisk the egg whites until very stiff and fold into the mousse. Stir in some finely chopped roast hazelnuts if liked. Put the mousse into a serving dish and return to the fridge to set. Sprinkle the top with grated chocolate topping. Delicious!

◄

"We may live without poetry, music and art
We may live without conscience and live without heart
We may live without friends; we may live without books
But civilised man cannot live without cooks".
Owen Meredith

CHOCOLATE ECLAIRS

MAKES ABOUT 10

1 quantity Choux Pastry (see page 83)
1 quantity Cream Filling (see **Note** and see page 84)

1 quantity Chocolate Topping (see page 85)

Prepare the choux pastry and put into a piping bag with a large nozzle. Pipe either round or long shapes on to a greased baking sheet, spacing well apart. Cook in a very hot oven, 240°C/475°F/Gas 9, for about 15 minutes (see **Note**).

Leave the risen choux to cool, then fill with the cream filling and dip the eclairs in chocolate topping to coat.

Note Always preheat the oven – this is particularly important when baking choux pastry.

Note When making the cream filling for the eclairs, use 1½ pints soya milk instead of just ½ pint, so giving a thinner cream.

◄

RASPBERRY ICE CREAM WITH RASPBERRY SAUCE

1 quantity Raspberry Ice Cream (see page 70)

1 quantity Raspberry Sauce (see page 22)

Make the ice cream and freeze. Meanwhile, make the sauce and leave to cool. Serve the sauce either poured over the ice cream or separately in a jug.

◄

A few of our experiments were greeted with "YUK" from Sophie.

STRIPED JELLY WITH FRUIT

6 teaspoons gelatine (sufficient to set 2 pints liquid)

2 pints sugar-free apple juice

red and green vegetable colouring

red and green fruits of choice

Sprinkle the gelatine on to ½ pint of the apple juice in a heatproof bowl. Leave until it becomes spongy, then stand the bowl in a pan of simmering water until the gelatine is completely dissolved.

Add the remaining apple juice and mix well. Colour 1 pint with red colouring and 1 pint with green colouring.

Put a little of one colour jelly into a jelly mould and leave to set in the fridge. Add a little of the second colour and leave to set in the fridge. Continue the layers, making sure that each layer in turn is completely set.

This jelly should be left overnight to become really firm before attempting to turn it out. Turn out the jelly and surround with red and green fruit.

◀

BIRTHDAY CAKE

3 oz creamed coconut

2 tablespoons boiling water

8 oz Granose margarine

2 oz Dietade Fruit Sugar

3 oz dates, minced

2 teaspoons almond essence

4 teaspoons mixed spice

2 teaspoons grated nutmeg

6 large eggs

8 oz plain flour

3 lb mixed raisins, sultanas and currants

a small amount of sugar-free apple juice

8 quantities sugar-free Marzipan (see pages 85 and 86)

Grate the coconut and mix with 2 tablespoons boiling water. Cream the margarine with the fructose, coconut and minced dates. Add the almond essence and spices. Add the eggs, one at a time, beating well after each addition. Fold in the flour and fruit. If the mixture is too stiff, add a little fruit juice and put into a greased and lined 10 inch tin. If possible leave to stand overnight before baking.

Bake in a cool oven, 140°C/275°F/Gas 1, for about 3–4 hours. Turn out the cake and brush with a little fruit juice. Decorate the top of the cake with sugar-free marzipan and add a cake frill.

Note For the top of Sophie's Birthday Cake, Ann made an icing sugar plaque which was a picture of Sophie's favourite things. We removed the plaque and keep it as a memento of the Birthday. These plaques keep for years and look lovely on a wall or dresser.

INDEX